The Daily Express

The Daily Express and Kogan Page have j... practical guides offering no-nonsense advice on a wide range of financial, legal and business topics.

Whether you want to manage your money better, make more money, get a new business idea off the ground – and make sure it's legal – there's a Daily Express Guide for you.

Titles published so far are:

Great Ideas for Making Money
Niki Chesworth

Your Money
How to Make the Most of it
Niki Chesworth

Buying a Property Abroad
Niki Chesworth

You and the Law
A Simple Guide to All Your Legal Problems
Susan Singleton

How to Cut Your Tax Bill Without Breaking the Law (Second Edition)
Grant Thornton, Chartered Accountants

Be Your Own Boss
How to Set Up a Successful Small Business
David McMullan

Readymade Business Letters That Get Results
Jim Douglas

The Woman's Guide to Finance
Ruth Sunderland

Buying Your First Franchise
G R Clarke

The Daily Express Guide to Investment
Virginia Blackburn

How to Succeed as a Network Marketeer
David Barber

A Guide for Small Business
Neil Johnson

Available from all good bookshops, or to obtain further information please contact the publishers at the address below:

Kogan Page Ltd
120 Pentonville Rd
LONDON N1 9JN
Tel: 0171-278 0433
Fax: 0171-837 6348

Daily Express

THE WOMAN'S GUIDE TO FINANCE

How to Manage all Your Money Matters

RUTH SUNDERLAND

KOGAN PAGE

Kogan Page Limited, the *Daily Express* and the author cannot assume legal responsibility for the accuracy of any particular statement in this work. No responsibility for loss or damage occasioned to any person acting or refraining from action as a result of the material in this publication can be accepted by the authors or publishers.

First published in 1995

Apart from any fair dealing for the purposes of research or private study, or criticism or review, as permitted under the Copyright, Designs and Patents Act, 1988, this publication may only be reproduced, stored or transmitted, in any form or by any means, with the prior permission in writing of the publishers, or in the case of reprographic reproduction in accordance with the terms of licences issued by the Copyright Licensing Agency. Enquiries concerning reproduction outside those terms should be sent to the publishers at the undermentioned address:

Kogan Page Limited
120 Pentonville Road
London N1 9JN

© Ruth Sunderland, 1995

British Library Cataloguing in Publication Data
A CIP record for this book is available from the British Library.

ISBN 0 7494 1338 7

Typeset by Saxon Graphics Ltd, Derby
Printed in England by Clays Ltd, St Ives plc

Contents

Introduction   9

1 Savings strategies   11
    Your savings aims   11
    Risk and reward   12
    How do you want to save?   13
    Do you need an income now?   14
    Making the most of savings   14

2 Choosing the best savings account   17
    Tax on savings   17
    Tax Exempt Special Savings Accounts   18
    National Savings   18
    More information   20

3 Making the stock market work for you   21
    Stocks and shares   21
    Unit and investment trusts   22
    Personal Equity Plans   23
    Endowment policies   24
    Friendly society plans   24
    Gilts   25
    More information   26

4 Tax matters   27
    Your tax-free allowances   27
    Allowances for older women and couples   28
    Income tax rates and bands   28
    Tax and your job   29
    Income tax on your savings and investments   29
    Capital gains tax   29
    Inheritance tax   30
    Anything to declare?   30
    Tax saving tips   31
    More information   32

5 Women at work — 33
- Equal pay for equal work — 33
- Equal opportunities — 35
- More information — 36

6 Buying your own home — 37
- Finding your new home — 37
- Picking the best mortgage — 38
- Variable or fixed rate? — 40
- Buying costs — 40
- Moving in — 41
- Joint mortgages — 42
- Coping with mortgage problems — 42
- More information — 43

7 Best ways to borrow money — 45
- Borrowing options — 45
- Counting the cost of credit — 46
- Short-term borrowings — 46
- Longer-term loans — 47
- Credit insurance — 47
- Joint borrowings — 48
- Bad references — 49
- Dealing with debt — 50
- More information — 51

8 Planning a rich retirement — 53
- Pensions from the state — 54
- Home responsibilities protection — 55
- State Earnings Related Pension Scheme — 56
- Equal pension ages — 56
- More information — 57

9 A pension with your job — 59
- Final salary schemes — 60
- Money purchase schemes — 60
- Hybrid schemes — 61

10 Personal pension plans — 63
- With-profits plans — 64
- Unit-linked plans — 64
- Deposit plans — 65
- Contracting out of SERPS — 65
- More information — 66

11 Building a man-sized pension — 67
What happens to my pension during a career break? — 67
Boosting your pension — 68
Early retirement — 69

12 Pension tips for job-changers — 71
Leaving your pension where it is — 71
Moving your pension to a new employer's scheme — 71
Transferring your pension to an insurance company — 72
More information — 73

13 Pensions and partners — 75
Pensions and divorce — 75
More information — 76

14 Living together — 79
Your home — 80
Making a will — 81
Insurance — 82
Tax and benefits — 82
Savings — 83
Pensions — 83
More information — 84

15 Money and marriage — 85
Preparing for the big day — 86
Tax and marriage — 86
Joint savings and investments — 87
Making a will — 88
Life cover is a must — 89
More information — 89

16 Financial family planning — 91
First steps — 91
Protecting your family — 92
Benefits for mothers — 92
School fees — 92
Saving for children — 93
More information — 94

17 Your maternity rights — 95
Maternity rights for working women — 95
Maternity benefits — 96
What you must tell your employer — and when — 97
More information — 98

8 / The woman's guide to finance

18 Combining work and home   99
    Part-time work   100
    Flexible working   100
    Working from home   101
    More information   102

19 Women mean business   105
    Your business plan   105
    Tax, VAT and financial planning   106
    More information   107

20 Dealing with divorce   109
    A financial settlement   109
    The family home   110
    Staying put   111
    Your income   111
    Tax matters   112
    Child support   112
    Money management   113
    More information   114

Appendix: more help and advice   117
    General financial planning guidance   117
    Financial advice   117
    Complaints   118
    Investments   119
    Compensation   120
    Benefits   121

Index   123

Introduction

No woman can afford to ignore the subject of finance.

The main theme of this book is the importance of financial independence, whether you are a single career woman or a mother with children.

Being in control of your finances brings you confidence and freedom. It means you can look forward to a more prosperous future.

And it means you — and your children — are less financially vulnerable if a crisis, such as divorce or separation, happens.

Although much of the information in general books on financial planning applies equally to both sexes, the different life patterns of men and women are often ignored.

Women's working lives tend to be more complicated than men's, because they often involve career breaks to bring up children and periods of part-time or flexible working.

This book aims to give financial planning advice for women taking into account those life changes. However, it is intended to be a springboard for women who want to learn the basics, not as an exhaustive manual. Details of where to get further information and help are included at the end of each chapter.

1
Savings strategies

Most women aim to save both for short-term peace of mind and to build up longer-term capital. There are thousands of savings products available — the only problem is choosing the one best suited to your needs. In the past, women did not enjoy full independence when it came to savings. Married women were forced to reveal their savings to their husbands as men were responsible for tax returns. Fortunately, that unfair situation ended in 1990, giving women complete privacy regarding their savings, however large or small.

Your savings aims

What are you saving for? Which type of savings plan is the best option depends on your aims, how long you want to save for, whether you might need to get your hands on the money in a hurry, and how much risk you are prepared to take.

All women should, however, consider three priorities.

- *Emergency funds*: It's well worth trying to build up a pot of emergency cash in a bank or building society account where you can get it at short notice, in case you suddenly find yourself faced with a big repair bill for your car or your home, for example.
- *Protect your family*: Make sure you have sufficient life insurance to provide for your dependants should anything happen. Remember that mums who stay at home to look after the family need insuring too — according to insurance company Legal & General it costs around £18,000 to buy in the cleaning, cooking and childcare services a mother provides each year.

Check that you have house buildings and contents cover and car insurance — it's a false economy to go without.
- *Planning for retirement*: Women need independent pensions. This is covered in more detail in the chapters on pensions later in the book.

Women should also consider how long to save for.
- *Short-term savings*: Short-term savings goals are aims you want to achieve within one or two years, such as a holiday, a new car, or even an expensive designer outfit. Here, your priority is to get the best return without locking your money in an account with heavy notice penalties. Stick to safe savings accounts like bank and building society accounts.
- *Medium term savings*: This is money you are setting aside for up to five years, and which you won't need in a hurry. Here, you can consider a range of tax-efficient accounts from banks, building societies and National Savings that are designed for savers who can tie their money up for five years. You will also be able to get better rates of return by putting your money into notice accounts. But remember that this does mean paying a penalty if you do take your money out before time.
- *Long-term savings*: This is money you can set aside for more than five years, for instance to finance a child's higher education, or to boost your retirement income. Here, you could consider savings linked to the stock market, which over time provide a better return than the building society. Possibilities include PEPs, unit trusts and investment trusts, along with friendly society plans and endowment policies.

Risk and reward

The more risk you are prepared to take with your savings, the greater the potential for reward. Although putting your money in the bank or building society is normally thought of as a safe investment, over the long term the buying power of your nest-egg is at risk from inflation. If you put £1000 in the building society now and spend the interest, you will still have £1000 capital in 20 years' time. But suppose prices rise at 5 per cent a year. Your £1000 will only be worth the equivalent of £377.

Research suggests women are more risk averse than men when it comes to investments. A Mintel report published this year showed only 8 per cent of women own unit trusts or stocks and shares. But this is likely to change as more women realise that long-term investments linked to the stock market stand a good chance of keeping up with inflation and of doing better than the bank or the building society. Over time, stock market investments can provide you with good capital growth and a rising income.

The disadvantage is that you have less security. With share-based investments like unit or investment trusts, the value of your capital can go down as well as up. Other options are endowment policies or friendly society plans, which smooth out the ups and downs of the stock market.

If you do want to put some cash into a riskier investment, always keep at least some of your money in a safe haven as a back-up. Investments linked to the stock market are most suitable for money you won't need to take out for five years or more.

How do you want to save?

Most savings accounts will accept a lump sum investment. If you are lucky enough to have come into a large windfall it's best to take independent financial advice on how to invest it. Saving regularly is a good habit to get into. It's a sensible idea to set up a standing order to your savings account — that way the money is paid in automatically, so you won't be tempted to break good resolutions and buy a new dress instead.

Some longer-term investments, including friendly society plans and endowment policies, are specially designed for regular savers. Others, including unit and investment trusts, have regular savings options.

Do you need an income now?

Most working women don't need to take an income from their savings immediately. They can reinvest the interest or dividends they earn so it is added to their capital. But if you have retired, you probably rely on your savings to boost your income.

Bank and building society variable savings rates go up and down in line with interest rates in the economy.

Alternatively, you can opt for a fixed rate investment, where the interest you get is guaranteed for a given period. These include gilts, and bank and building society fixed rate accounts. But buying a fixed rate investment is a gamble — if interest rates rise, you may lose out.

Stockmarket investments offer the potential of a rising income over time, though the dividends paid out may fall as well as rise.

Be sceptical of any product offering an income that seems too good to be true — because it probably is. Many so-called 'high income' investments are not really paying a high income at all — they are simply returning part of your capital.

Making the most of savings

An estimated £800 million is lost because savers leave their money in dead savings accounts. Banks and building societies often close down accounts to new investors in order to promote newer savings products paying tempting rates. When that happens, unsuspecting savers can be left earning very poor rates of interest — sometimes less than 1 per cent. Check with your bank or building society that you are not in an obsolete account, or switch to one which makes a commitment not to short-change savers. So far, only two building societies, the Leeds, which is merging with the Halifax, and the National & Provincial, have taken serious action to protect savers from losing out. They automatically move savers out of obsolete accounts into better ones. However, it has not yet been decided whether the Halifax will continue moving savers automatically to the best accounts after the merger. With any of the others, it's up to you to take the initiative.

Make sure you channel your money into tax-free investments such as friendly society plans, TESSAs, PEPs and National Savings Certificates. The Inland Revenue deducts 25 per cent automatically from most other savings income. But there are tax-breaks for non-taxpayers and those on lower rate. Women who don't work outside the home and other non-taxpayers should apply to receive their bank and building society interest without tax deducted — ask your local tax office for form IR110. Women working part-time and others who are only paying tax at the lower rate of 20 per cent can reclaim the 5 per cent difference from the Inland Revenue.

Married couples can save tax by switching investments into the name of the lower earning partner — see the chapters on tax and on money and marriage for more details. But high-achieving career wives should bear in mind that any transfers have to be outright gifts.

2
Choosing the Best Savings Account

Banks and building societies offer a wide range of savings accounts. When choosing an account, there are several questions to consider:

- What is the minimum investment?
- What are the rules on paying in more money?
- How easily can you get at your savings?
- How often is the interest paid?
- Is the interest fixed or variable?
- How much interest can you earn? Generally speaking, the longer you can tie your money up for, and the larger the amount you have to invest, the higher the interest rate.
  Many accounts have tiered rates, so the more money you invest, the better the return.
- Are you getting the best rate? Check the savings rate tables published in the money pages of national newspapers including Wednesday's *Daily Express*. Consider postal accounts, offered by several building societies. Because these accounts are cheap to run, they often pay better rates.

Tax on savings

Bank and building society income is taxed at your highest rate. Normally you receive the interest net of basic rate tax, so those on basic rate need do nothing more. Anyone who pays tax at the lower rate of 20 per cent can claim a refund, and higher rate taxpayers will have extra to pay. Non-taxpayers can reclaim the tax or even better, register to receive it gross.

Tax Exempt Special Savings Accounts

TESSAs are tax-free accounts run by banks and building societies, designed to run for five years. You can save up to £3000 in the first year and up to £1,800 in each of the next four years, provided you don't put in more than £9000 in total.

But even if you think you may want access to your savings before five years are up, a TESSA can still be a good bet, since they often pay good rates, and the most you stand to lose is the tax relief.

Minimum investments vary but many will accept regular monthly savings from £1 upwards. The maximum monthly saving allowed by the Inland Revenue is £150.

You are free to transfer your TESSA from one bank or building society to another, but there may be penalties. And some TESSA providers pay a bonus to savers who stay loyal for the full five years.

Under new rules announced in the 1994 Budget, when your TESSA matures, you can transfer up to £9000 into a new TESSA.

Tax: Tax-free.
Suitable for: Medium term savers. Especially good for well-paid women who can save higher rate tax on their investment, but a sensible option for anyone who wants to save tax-free.

National Savings

National Savings offers a range of accounts, including:

- *Granny Bonds:* The new Granny Bonds, launched at the start of 1994, are open to the over 65s. They pay a fixed rate of 7.5 per cent gross over five years. The minimum investment is £500 and the maximum is £20,000. Interest is paid into your bank or building society account each month. Capital withdrawals are subject to a 60-day interest penalty.
  Tax: Interest is paid with no tax taken off but you are liable for tax at your highest rate.
  Suitable for: Pensioners who want a fixed return and can tie

Choosing the best savings account / 19

up their money for five years. But the 65 lower age limit is a big drawback for many women who retired at 60.
- *First Option Bonds:* These are aimed at basic rate taxpayers. You can invest a minimum of £1000 up to a maximum of £250,000. The interest rate is 4.8 per cent net on sums up to £20,000 and 5.1 per cent on larger amounts, fixed for one-year. At the end of 12 months you can either cash in, or opt to reinvest at a new fixed one year rate. If you withdraw in the first year, you get no interest. After that if you cash in part-way through a year, you will only get half the normal rate for that year, so it's best to cash in on the bond's anniversary.
Tax: Interest is paid with basic rate tax taken off automatically. Non-taxpayers and lower rate taxpayers can reclaim tax, higher rate taxpayers have to pay more.
- *NS Certificates:* The current 42nd issue pays a guaranteed five-year return of 5.85 per cent. Minimum investment is £100, maximum is £10,000, but you can reinvest up to £20,000 of matured certificates. Returns are reduced if you cash in early, and there is no interest at all if you cash in during the first year.
Tax: Tax-free.
- *Suitable for:* Medium-term lump sum savers, well-paid women who want to save higher rate tax.
- *Index-linked Certificates:* Similar to ordinary certificates, except that the current 8th Issue pays a return of 3 per cent on top of inflation, guaranteed for five years.
Tax: Tax-free.
Suitable for: Medium-term lump sum savers worried about inflation, well-paid women who are higher rate taxpayers.
- *Capital Bonds:* The minimum investment is £100 and the maximum is £250,000. The current rate is 7.75 per cent gross, fixed for five years, though the rate is reduced if you cash in early.
Tax: Taxable, but non-taxpayers receive interest gross after five-years. Taxpayers must pay tax on the interest each year,

even though they won't receive it for five years.
Suitable for: Medium-term lump sum savers; non taxpayers; a good investment for children.

- *Children's Bonus Bonds:* These are an ideal investment if you want to put some money away for children or grandchildren, because they pay a high tax-free rate of interest. They can be bought by anyone aged 16 or over for a child under 16. Once purchased, they can be held until the youngster is 21.

    Minimum investment is £25, maximum £1000. The interest rate is 7.85 per cent, guaranteed for five years.
    Tax: Tax-free.
    Suitable for: Mums, grandmothers, aunts, godmothers or anyone else who wants to invest for kids.

More information

National & Provincial Building Society produces special savings leaflets for women as part of its Financial Services for Women initiative. Tel: 0800 600 200.

3
Making the stock market work for you

The stock market has a reputation as a casino where only the professional gamblers stand a chance of winning. But investing in stocks and shares is well within the reach of the man — or woman — in the street. In fact, you are probably a stock market investor already without even knowing it. If you have a pension or an endowment policy, your money is indirectly going into stocks and shares.

Provided you spread your risks and invest for the long term, putting money into the stock market can be both profitable and enjoyable.

Stocks and shares

Many women have already dabbled in the stock market by buying shares in privatisation issues such as BT or British Gas. Buying shares can be risky — but if you are astute enough to pick the right companies, you can make good profits.

- Experts recommend you do not invest directly in shares unless you have at least £20,000 at your disposal to channel into 5–10 different companies. That is around the minimum sum that will give you a decent spread of risk — if you put too much into one single share, you are very vulnerable if the price falls.
- It is not worth investing small amounts in shares because stockbroker's commission can wipe out all your profits. Smaller investors are normally better off sticking to unit or investment trusts.

Government privatisations are really the only exception, because there are no buying charges and the price is usually pitched so investors stand to make a profit. The only problem is there is now very little left to privatise.
- If you do have the wherewithal to build up a share portfolio, or if you inherited one from someone else, your first decision is whether to manage it yourself or to hand it over to a professional manager.
- Running your own portfolio profitably is hard work — though some women have done so highly successfully. You will have to spend a great deal of time learning about investments by reading background material and scouring the financial press. Most investors of this type use a low-cost stockbroker service, which is designed simply to carry out your buy and sell instructions without giving you any advice.
- You can opt for a stockbroking service with advice, which will be more expensive. With this option, you will still be responsible for making the ultimate dealing decisions, and for valuing the portfolio each year and handling the income and capital gains tax due.
- If you have a large portfolio, you can choose a portfolio management service where everything is done for you. Some managers insist on making all the investment decisions themselves — others allow you the final say.
- Share dividends come with tax at 20 per cent deducted at source. Basic and lower rate taxpayers don't have to pay any more, but higher rate taxpayers must top up their payment to 40 per cent. Non-taxpayers can reclaim the tax. Capital gains tax at your highest tax rate is payable on profits. But you have an annual exemption of £6000 in the 1995/6 tax year.

Unit and investment trusts

Unit and investment trusts are most suitable for long-term investors who are prepared to take the risk of losing some or all of their money in return for greater potential rewards than the building society. Your money is pooled with that of other investors in the trust, and invested in a wide range of shares and other assets, so it spreads your risk.

- You can cash in without penalty whenever you choose. But it is best not to put money you may need in a hurry into the stock market — you may lose out if you are forced to sell at a point when prices are low.
- Most unit trusts and investment trust savings schemes set minimum lump sum investments of £500–1000 or £30–50 per month. Invesment trust savings schemes can be particularly good value in terms of charges — most make a minimal charge of 0.2 per cent. With unit trusts, there is normally a 5–6 per cent initial charge, and you will normally have to pay annual management charges of 1–1.5 per cent.

Personal Equity Plans

Up to £6000 of UK or European Union shares can be tax-sheltered in a Personal Equity Plan each tax year. The £6,000 limit also applies to unit and investment trusts provided at least half of the trust's assets are in the UK or the European Union. In the 1994 Budget, it was announced that company bonds, convertibles and preference shares were also eligible for the full £6000 PEP allowance. These sound complicated, but are basically investments paying a fixed income, and are generally somewhat less risky than shares. However, they are not totally safe building society-type investments either, so ask your PEP seller for a full explanation of the risks. Many unit and investment trust PEPs allow regular contributions from £30–50 per month.

- Unit and investment trusts are tax-free in a PEP, otherwise income is paid net of lower rate tax. Non-taxpayers and lower rate taxpayers can reclaim the tax, higher rate taxpayers must pay extra. Profits are liable to capital gains tax, though there is an annual exemption of £6000 in the 1995/6 tax year.

- These investments are risky, but offer the chance of higher rewards than the building society. They are suitable for long-term savers who are prepared to take a risk and well paid women who want to save higher rate tax.

Endowment policies

Endowment policies are a long-term option for regular savers, with annual returns in the region of 12–13 per cent. You commit yourself to saving a set regular sum each month for a given period; usually ten or 25 years.

- With-profits endowments are a relatively safe way of gaining exposure to stock market growth potential. Life company funds invest in a mixture of shares, property and fixed interest investments, and your return comes in the form of regular bonuses, which, once added, cannot be removed. There is also a terminal bonus when the policy matures.
- Proceeds from an endowment are tax-free, though the fund in which your premiums are invested is taxable. The biggest problem with these policies is that if you want to cash in before the end of the term — as a large proportion of policy holders do — you will get a very low surrender value. In the first five years, it could be less than you have put in.
- Endowments are a relatively safe way of investing in the stock market. But because much of the return comes in the form of the maturity bonus, your total return is uncertain right until the end.

Friendly society plans

Friendly society plans are tax-free, and operate in a similar way to an endowment policy, with similar returns. The most you can invest is £25 per month or £270 a year into a plan, designed to last ten years. Beware of cashing in early, though, since the returns can be heavily reduced.

Friendly society plans are a very tax-efficient way mothers, grandmothers and aunts can invest for a child. Many friendly societies offer 'half-plans' for those who want to save for more than one child.

They are suitable for long-term small savers, mums, grandmothers, aunts and godmothers or anyone else who wants to invest for children.

Gilts

Gilts are basically IOUs from the government. They pay a fixed rate of return, or coupon, and the government guarantees to repay a fixed capital value, normally £100, when they mature. For instance, Treasury 12 per cent 1998 means the coupon is 12 per cent and the government will give you back £100 in 1998.

- Gilts can be bought and sold on the stock market, and you are unlikely to pay exactly £100, so the actual rate you receive won't usually be the same as the coupon.
- If you keep a gilt until it matures, you know exactly what return you will get. If you sell before maturity, you could make a gain — or a loss. Bear in mind that if you pay more than £100 for your gilts and keep them to maturity, you are locking into a capital loss.
- You can buy gilts easily and cheaply through the National Savings Stock Register in major post offices. The minimum commission for purchases is £5 from February 1995 — much cheaper than a stockbroker. You can also invest in index-linked gilts, which offer some protection against inflation. Interest on gilts bought through the Post Office is paid gross but is taxable. Capital gains are tax-free.
   There is no risk to your capital unless you sell before the gilts mature.
- Gilts are suitable for investors who want a fixed income and guaranteed capital return.

More information

You can get more information about unit trusts from:

The Association of Unit Trusts and Investment Funds
65 Kingsway
London WC2B 6TD
Tel: 0181-207 1361

More detail on investment trusts is available from:

The Association of Investment Trust Companies
Park House
6th Floor
16 Finsbury Circus
London EC2M 7JJ
Tel: 0171-588 5347

You can obtain a list of private client stockbrokers from:

The Association of Private Client Stockbrokers and Investment Managers
112 Middlesex Street
London E1 7HY

The wider share ownership organisation ProShare offers a range of information services to private sharebuyers:

ProShare
Library Chambers
13–14 Basinghall Street
London EC2V 5BQ
Tel: 0171-600 0984

4
Tax matters

Tax is an inescapable part of your finances. The tax rules affect your pay, your savings income, your mortgage and any profits you make on investments. All women, whether married, single, separated or divorced, are responsible for their own tax affairs in the eyes of the Inland Revenue. In the chapters on savings and investments, tax-free investments have been pointed out. But here, we look at the workings of the tax system, and how you might make some tax savings.

Your tax-free allowances

The tax year runs from April to April. Each tax year you are given a tax allowance. This is the amount of income you can receive before you start to pay tax. Everyone has a 'Personal Allowance', and you may have other allowances, such as a Married Couple's Allowance or Additional Personal Allowance. If your income is less than your allowances, you are a non-taxpayer.

For 1995/6, the allowances are:

   Personal Allowance: £3525
   Married Couple's Allowance   £1720

- The Married Couple's Allowance is automatically given to your husband. But you can elect to share it equally between you by informing the authorities you wish to do so before the end of the previous tax year — you don't need your husband's permission to do this. If you both agree, you can have the full Married Couple's Allowance yourself.
- Tax relief on the Married Couple's Allowance drops to 15 per cent in the 1995/6 tax year, so the MCA is worth £258.

- If you are single, separated or divorced and have a child or children living with you, you are entitled to an Additional Personal Allowance of £1720. Relief is given in the same way as the Married Couples' Allowance. Your child must be under 16, or in full-time education at university, college or school.

Allowances for older women and couples

- Over 65s are entitled to higher personal allowances. In 1995/6 these are:

Personal allowance age	65–74	£4630
	over 75	£4800
Married Couple's Allowance	65–74	£2995
	over 75	£3035

- For single women and widows, your higher Personal Allowance is reduced by £1 for each £2 of income you receive above £14,600 in the 1994/5 tax year. But your allowance will not be allowed to fall below the basic Personal Allowance.
- Higher Married Couple's Allowances are granted on the basis of the age of the older spouse in the tax year. Husband and wife each have their own £14,600 income limit.
- There are special tax reliefs for widows. In the tax year your husband dies, you receive the Married Couple's Allowance. You can also claim the Widow's Bereavement Allowance — the same sum as the Married Couple's Allowance — in the year after his death.

Income tax rates and bands

Any taxable income between £3201 and £24,300 in the 1995/6 tax year is taxed at the basic rate of 25 per cent. Taxable income of more than £24,300 is taxed at 40 per cent in the 1995/6 tax year, and the first £3200 of taxable income is taxed at 20 per cent.

The tax rates and bands for 1994/5 are:

Taxable income	Rate
Up to £3200	20 %
£3201–£24,300	25 %
More than £24,300	40 %

Tax and your job

- If you work for an employer, you will usually be taxed through the Pay As You Earn or PAYE system. Your employer deducts the tax you have to pay out of your wages or salary before you receive them.
- Each tax year, the Inland Revenue issues you with a PAYE code, telling your employer how much of your pay is free of tax. The last number is missed off. So, for instance, if your PAYE code is 352L, it tells your employer you receive the personal allowance, and should get £3525 of tax-free pay.

Income tax on your savings and investments

- Interest on bank or building society savings accounts is paid net of basic rate tax, but it is taxable at your highest rate. If you are a 25 per cent taxpayer, your liability is fully covered. Higher rate taxpayers must pay the extra 15 per cent. Lower rate taxpayers can reclaim the 5 per cent they have overpaid, and non-taxpayers can register to receive the income with no tax deducted.
- Dividends from shares, unit trusts and investment trusts are paid with tax of 20 per cent already deducted. If you are a non-taxpayer, you can claim the tax back. If you are a lower or basic rate taxpayer, you have no further tax to pay, but if you are a higher rate taxpayer, you must pay a further 20 per cent tax.
- If you and your husband have joint savings or investments, the tax authorities assume you receive half the income each.

Capital gains tax

If you make a profit when you sell certain assets, such as shares or a valuable painting, you may be liable for capital gains tax.

Capital gains tax may be payable when you dispose of an asset, whether you sell it or give it away, so you can't avoid the tax by making presents of your assets.

Fortunately, many of your main assets are exempt from capital gains tax, including:

- your only or main home;
- gifts between husband and wife;
- private motor cars;
- bank and building society savings and National Savings accounts;
- betting winnings;
- gilts.

You also have an annual gains tax exemption — £6000 in the 1995/6 tax year. Husband and wife each have their own exemption.

Any profits above the exemption from shares, unit trusts or investment trusts are added to your taxable income and taxed at your highest rate.

Inheritance tax

Many people underestimate their assets and wrongly assume that inheritance tax, charged at 40 per cent if the value of your estate exceeds £154,000 (the nil rate band in the 1995/6 tax year) does not affect them. So if your estate, including the family home, is worth £204,000, your potential inheritance tax bill is £50,000 × 40% = £20,000.

Married couples each have their own £154,000 nil rate band.

Anything to declare?

If you receive a tax return, you *must* fill it in fully and honestly, and return it promptly, otherwise you may be charged interest and penalties.

Most women who are basic rate taxpayers and are taxed under PAYE will often not be sent a tax return.

But if you have other income, for instance from a second job or from letting out a property, it is your responsibility to notify the tax authorities, whether or not they send you a return.

Tax saving tips

- If you are a non-taxpayer ask for form R85 at your bank or building society so you can register to receive interest on your savings with no tax deducted.
- If you are a lower rate taxpayer, you can reclaim the 5 per cent tax overpaid on savings interest. See leaflet IR110, *A Guide for People with Savings*, available from your local tax office.
- Married couples should consider transferring income-producing assets into the name of the partner paying the lowest rate of tax. For instance, if you are a 40 per cent taxpayer and your husband is paying the basic rate of 25 per cent, transferring some of your savings into his name could save 15 per cent tax. But the assets you transfer become his — you cannot attach strings to the transfer.
- Always check your tax code — the Revenue can make mistakes leaving you paying too much tax.
- Make the most of tax-free savings and investment opportunities. These include:
  - National Savings certificates and index-linked certificates;
  - TESSAs;
  - Personal Equity Plans.

  More details of these are given in the chapters on savings and investments.
- Plan the disposal of your assets to minimise capital gains tax bills. For instance, if you have a share investment you want to keep, but it is showing a profit of £10,000 and you are worried about the gains tax, you could 'bed and breakfast' some shares, that is sell them and then buy them back straightaway. If you sold enough shares to realise a profit of £5000 this tax year, there would be no gains tax to pay because it is within your £6000 tax-free allowance. Do the

same thing next year, and you have eliminated the potential bill.
- You can reduce potential inheritance tax bills by making a tax-efficient will. Gifts made within your lifetime can also reduce the bill. Most gifts are Potentially Exempt Transfers — there is no tax to pay provided you live for seven years after making the gift.

Some gifts are totally tax-free, including:
- a gift of up to £3000 to any one person;
- gifts from parents of up to £5000 to a child on their marriage, and up to £2500 from grandparents;
- an unlimited number of small gifts of up to £250 each year.

More information

National & Provincial building society Financial Services for Women publishes useful booklets, *Understanding the Tax System Guide for Women* and the *Taxation Guide for Women*. Tel: 0800 600200.

Your local tax office should be able to help with queries — the number is listed in the telephone directory.

5
Women at work

In the bad old days women had to choose between a career and a family. Now, whether through choice or economic necessity, most women have to juggle both. Changes in society mean women are more likely to be involved in paid employment than ever before. Many companies are cutting back on traditional male full-time posts and replacing them with part-time positions likely to be filled by women. In many households, women are becoming the main or only breadwinners.

By the start of the 1990s, women in the UK had the second highest rate of participation in the labour force of any European country, and the highest number of women in employment. Now, around 65 per cent of women work outside the home, and women account for one in four of the self-employed, according to Employment Department statistics.

It means the majority of women will need to tackle a range of financial issues connected with paid employment, including maternity benefits, your rights when it comes to equal pay for equal work, and combining a career with a family.

Equal pay for equal work

It would be very rare to find a man being paid more than a woman for doing exactly the same job nowadays. Equal Pay regulations brought in in 1984 state that a woman can claim 'equal pay for work of equal value' to a man working for the same employer. The Sex Discrimination Act of 1975 (along with subsequent amendments in 1986 and 1989) makes it unlawful for employers to discriminate against anyone on the grounds of their sex. The Act covers recruitment, training, promotion, dismissal and retirement.

But the great male/female pay divide still persists. Average full-time female earnings are currently just 79 per cent of the average male wage, according to the Employment Department. Even at the top, figures from researchers at Sedgwick Noble Lowndes show female executives earn an average of £54,836 a year, 23 per cent less than the average male executive on £67,371.

There is no easy answer on how individual women can make sure their work is not undervalued. Training and working for relevant professional qualifications should help boost your salary and open more options on the job market. Contact your local Training and Enterprise Council, or speak to your manager or company training department.

If you are a victim of sex discrimination at work, you can take your case to an Industrial Tribunal. Go to your local Employment Service office and ask for application form IT1 or IT(Scot) in Scotland.

Sexual harassment is now recognised as a factor that can hold back women at work, stopping them from doing their job and lowering morale. The Equal Opportunities Commission launched new guidelines for dealing with it in October 1994 after complaints of harassment rose by 300 to 793 during 1993.

The European Commission Code of Conduct defines sexual harassment as: 'Unwanted conduct of a sexual nature based on sex affecting the dignity of men and women at work. This can include unwelcome physical, verbal or non verbal conduct.'

In other words, it can include lewd remarks or glances, requests for sexual favours and physical contact.

Under the Sex Discrimination Act, the employer is liable for discriminatory acts by employees whilst at work. There is no limit to the sums that can be awarded in cases taken to industrial tribunals.

Equal opportunities

Women still have a long way to go to achieve the same career status as men. According to Employment Department statistics, out of 144,000 managers of large companies, only 8 per cent are female. The ratio of men to women holding public appointments is 3 : 1. In professions such as medicine, the law and education the picture is no better. Fewer than 15 per cent of medical consultants are women, even though half of all medical students are female. Only 3 per cent of professors and principal lecturers at universities are female, and women account for just 5 per cent of circuit judges.

But fortunately, that's beginning to change. Some employers are streets ahead of others when it comes to the treatment of female staff — it's worth researching if you are job hunting. Companies that have signed the Opportunity 2000 initiative launched by John Major in October 1991 have committed themselves to the aim of 'increasing the quality and quantity of women's participation in the workforce'. They include Abbey National, Boots the Chemist, Sainsburys, several universities, BT and WH Smith.

Opportunity 2000 now has 275 members, accounting for more than a quarter of the UK workforce. It claims significant successes since launch. Amongst its members, women hold 25 per cent of managerial posts, more than double the percentage in UK top companies as a whole. At director level, women account for 8 per cent of posts amongst Opportunity 2000 members, compared with less than 3 per cent elsewhere.

When taken seriously, policies to advance women can be highly successful. For instance, Barclays Bank, an Opportunity 2000 member, has doubled the number of female managers in a decade by bringing in a range of woman-friendly working practices, including career break schemes for women and men after the birth of a baby, emergency carer's leave, job-sharing and term-time only contracts.

More information

The Equal Opportunities Commission aims to eliminate sex discrimination at work. It publishes a leaflet, *Sexual Harassment: What You Can Do About It*, available from:

EOC
Overseas House
Quay Street
Manchester M3 3HN
Tel: 0161-833 9244
Price £1.

6
Buying your own home

Your home is likely to be your biggest financial asset as well as a place to live. So you are not only trying to find a dream dwelling — or as near to it as possible — but also aiming to make a sound investment.

Because of the trend towards later marriages and greater female earning power, more single women are buying a home on their own than ever before, rather than waiting until they marry or move in with a partner.

But whether you are buying a home as a single person or with a partner, friend, or relative, it pays to be clued up on the costs and on your responsibilities as a mortgage holder.

Finding your new home

Your first step towards finding a new home is to sign up with an estate agent.

- Be specific on the size and type of property you are looking for, which areas you would prefer, and your price range.
- Don't waste time viewing properties you know will not be suitable — but be prepared to be flexible. You are unlikely to find complete perfection.
- When you find a property you want to buy, make an offer through the estate agent.
- Estate agents act for the seller, not the buyer. That means it is the agent's main job to persuade you to buy at the highest possible price. Don't be afraid to bargain — sellers usually set their asking price higher than they actually expect to receive.
- It is a criminal offence for estate agents to make false or misleading statements about a property offered for sale. But

they will still try to put on the best possible gloss.
- Don't be influenced by superficial factors such as decoration or attractive fittings — they don't add much value and you are likely to want to redecorate anyway.
- Consider whether your new home is convenient for shops, good schools, public transport, parks, recreational facilities and so on.
- Be clear about exactly what the selling price includes. For instance, will the seller be leaving behind fixtures such as fireplaces, and fittings such as carpets and shelves?
- Is the property freehold or leasehold? Many flats are leasehold. Be wary of buying anything with a short lease — seventy years is a good rule of thumb. Don't go below it unless the property is unusual or very desirable.

Picking the best mortgage

Single women can usually borrow up to three times their salary and couples can take a loan of up to two and a half times joint incomes. Try to leave yourself some money in hand each month in case interest rates rise. Nowadays it is unusual for borrowers to be granted a 100 per cent mortgage — you will normally have to find a deposit of at least 5 per cent.

The tax relief on mortgage interest, known as MIRAS or Mortgage Interest Relief at Source, is being progressively cut. From April 1995 it will go down to 15 per cent on interest on the first £30,000 of your home loan.

Any high street bank or building society will advise you on mortgages. The two best known types of loan are the repayment and the endowment mortgages. You also have to consider whether you want to take out a fixed rate mortgage or one where the interest rate varies.

Repayment mortgages are the simplest type. Your monthly payments are used to reduce the capital as well as the interest. At first, the capital goes down slowly, but at the end of the term, usually 25 years, you will have repaid the loan in full.

With an endowment mortgage, you pay interest only throughout the life of the loan, and you also pay premiums to an endowment policy, which you hope will give you enough to repay the loan at the end of its term, and perhaps leave you with a tax-free lump sum as well.

These are the most popular types of home loan. But remember you will pay high commission and costs on the endowment policy. Never cash in an endowment when you move — the return will be very poor. You can always take out another policy to top up if you need to cover a larger mortgage.

Homebuyers can also take out a pension or a PEP mortgage. Pension mortgages are similar to endowment-linked loans, except it is your pension that is used as backing. They are very tax-efficient for higher rate taxpayers, because you receive tax relief at your highest rate on contributions to the pension. But you have to pay off the home loan out of your pension lump sum, which will reduce your income when you retire.

With a PEP mortgage, you make monthly payments into a tax-free Personal Equity Plan, which invests in unit or investment trusts or shares, and pay interest only off your mortgage. Again, you hope your PEP will produce enough to pay off the loan at the end of the term.

PEPs are more flexible than endowments because you can cash in at any time without penalty. It means if your plan performs well, you can pay off your mortgage early, and save yourself a chunk of interest. But they are also more risky, because they are linked to the stock market.

Tables showing the best mortgage rates are printed in the personal finance sections of newspapers. The *Daily Express* publishes rates every Wednesday.

Be careful when taking out a tempting discount offer, though. There is often a catch. The discount may run for a short period only, there may be heavy penalties if you have to move mortgages within a given time, often three years, and you may have to take out expensive insurance policies through the lender to qualify for the cheap rate.

Variable or fixed rate?

Fixed rate mortgages, as their name suggests, set your repayments at a guaranteed rate for a given period, normally from one to five years. With a variable rate loan, your instalments go up and down according to interest rate movements.

One advantage of a fixed loan is that you know exactly how much you will be paying over the term, and you will not suffer if interest rates go up. But you could lose out if you fix your repayments and then interest rates go down. You will also have to pay an arrangement fee of £200–£300, and there are heavy penalties if you want to change mortgage before the fixed term has ended.

Buying costs

There are a whole host of hidden extras. According to the Abbey National, fees on a £50,000 home with a 95 per cent mortgage add up to around £1500 at 1994 prices. Make sure you budget for:

- A deposit of at least 5 per cent of the property value
- Loan arrangement fees of £200–300 on fixed-rate mortgages.
- A report on the condition of the property and valuation, costing around £260 on a £50,000 home. If the property is old or unusual, get a full structural survey.
- Find a qualified solicitor to handle the conveyancing and paperwork. Legal fees vary depending on your area and the solicitor you use. Abbey National estimates the cost at £440 on a £50,000 property.
- Local search at £50 and £100 land registry fee.
- Mortgage indemnity premiums for those borrowing more than three quarters of the property value — about £700 on a £50,000 purchase.
- Stamp duty of 1 per cent on homes bought for more than £60,000.
- Buyers will also need to set aside some money for removal

expenses, redecoration and new furniture. Check the removal firm has adequate insurance in case of breakages.
- Don't forget monthly outgoings such as council tax, gas and electricity bills and water rates. Ask the present owners about average bills and costs.
- You will have to pay for compulsory house buildings and home contents insurance premiums each month as well as your mortgage instalments. It is also sensible to take out an insurance policy to cover your monthly payments if you have an accident, fall ill or lose your job. Until October 1995, income support claimants receive up to half their mortgage interest from the DSS in the first 16 weeks after claiming and then the full interest after that, up to a maximum mortgage of £125,000. From October 1995, new borrowers will not receive any help for the first nine months, and the mortgage ceiling has been cut to £100,000. So it's more important than ever to take out your own insurance.

Moving in

Once your survey has been done, your mortgage agreed and your solicitor has completed various searches, you should be ready to exchange contracts. At this stage, you pay over your deposit and you are committed to buy.

The home actually changes ownership some time after exchange, normally about 28 days.

Your solicitor arranges for the mortgage money to be paid to the seller's solicitor and you can then collect the keys. This is known as completion.

When you move, you will need to contact the gas, electricity and telephone companies to transfer the accounts into your name. You will also need to inform friends, your employer, your doctor and dentist that you have moved. If you have savings or investments, remember to notify the provider of your new address, along with the DVLA if you drive a car.

Joint mortgages

Couples buying a home together should sit down and agree the proportion of the home loan and bills each will pay. It is also worth considering how you want to deal with the investment plans you are using to back the mortgage. For instance, taking out a joint endowment can cause problems if you split up, as the policy may have to be cashed in, often incurring big penalties. But there is no reason why each partner cannot take out their own policy or PEP to back their slice of the mortgage, and simply carry on with it in the event of a break-up.

You also need to consider the question of ownership of the home. Most married couples are 'joint tenants', which means they both own the whole property jointly. If one or other dies, the whole property automatically passes to the survivor, whatever is written in the will.

The other form of ownership is to be 'tenants in common.' Here, the interests of each partner are fixed, usually 50:50, but couples can agree on a different proportion. If one partner dies, their share goes into their estate and can be left to whoever they please.

Women buying a home with a husband or partner should be aware that when they take out a joint mortgage, both parties are potentially liable for the full debt. So if your husband or partner cannot or will not pay, the lender may well chase you for the money. Your ownership arrangements are irrelevant — even if you only own 30 per cent of your home as a tenant in common, you are responsible for the full mortgage instalments.

Coping with mortgage problems

If you run into difficulty with your repayments because you or your partner lose your job or fall ill, the golden rule is to inform your lender straightaway. Most lenders will be reasonably sympathetic. If you have a mortgage protection policy, inform your insurer as soon as possible.

Never hand in your keys assuming you can then walk away from your debts — you can't. Even after your home has been repossessed, the lender can pursue you for the money you owe. Try to co-operate with your lender, and you have a much better chance of keeping your home.

You can seek help from your local Citizen's Advice Bureau or Money Advice Centre. Look in the telephone directory for their numbers.

More information

The National Debtline, tel: 0121-359 8501, specialises in advice and information on housing and other debts.

The *Rights Guide for Home Owners*, a book published by housing charity SHAC and the Child Poverty Action Group, is extremely informative on your financial rights and what to do if you get into mortgage difficulty. It is available from:

SHAC Publications
Kingsbourne House
229–231 High Holborn
London WC1V 7DA
Tel: 0171-404 7447
Price £10.95 (including postage and packing).

7
Best ways to borrow money

Sensible borrowing forms part of most people's financial planning. But the plethora of credit options available can be confusing.

Few families have a strong enough cash flow to cope with making all their major purchases out of income or savings, so identifying the best way to borrow is essential if you don't want to end up paying over the odds for your credit purchases.

If you do have savings, it will generally make sense to use them rather than take out a loan, because the interest you will earn on your savings is less than you will have to pay on borrowings.

Borrowing options

To work out which type of credit is most suitable, you need to think about how much you want to borrow, for how long, and how much repayment flexibility you would like.

If you need short-term credit, to cover a cash emergency, for instance, your best bet is probably an authorised overdraft. For small purchases, where convenience and flexibility over payment are at a premium, go for a credit card.

You may consider a personal loan where repayments are spread over periods of six months to five years for more expensive purchases such as a new car, and for amounts of £10,000 or over, the cheapest way to borrow is normally by taking out a loan secured on your home. But remember your home is at risk if you fail to keep up the repayments.

Counting the cost of credit

It is not easy to compare the true cost of different kinds of borrowing. The law requires lenders to quote Annual Percentage Rates or APRs on most types of loan. APRs take into account the flat interest rate, the amount borrowed and additional costs.

Banks are not forced by law to quote APRs on current account overdrafts. Many now quote an EAR or Equivalent Annual Rate instead — make sure you check on what other charges are levied.

Short-term borrowings

Credit cards are a very flexible and easy way to borrow. You can use them simply as a convenient payment method, and pay your bill in full at the end of each month, which with some cards will give you up to eight weeks' free credit, or you can spread the cost of purchases over several months. You can pay as much or as little as you want each month, subject to a minimum, usually 5 per cent of your balance, or £5. Most now levy an annual fee of £10–12.

But the rates of interest are quite high if you continuously run a debt on your card. It's worth shopping around for the cheapest interest rate — you don't have to take the card offered by your own bank.

Store cards work very much like credit cards, but can only be used in one chain of shops. With the honourable exceptions of John Lewis and Marks & Spencer, which offer good rates, these are best avoided. Many charge very high interest rates.

Stores also offer interest-free credit deals on selected items — naturally, these are a very good idea, though you will normally have to put down a deposit, and the repayment times on quite major purchases can be as short as six months.

Arranging an overdraft on your current account is a flexible and convenient way to borrow for shorter periods. But it is not necessarily any cheaper than using a credit card or cheap store card, and you need to watch out for fees and charges. Be careful not to slip into the red inadvertently, or to exceed an agreed overdraft limit.

Interest rates on unauthorised overdrafts are high — and so are other charges.

Longer-term loans

Personal loans from banks or building societies can be a good way to finance larger purchases such as a car, where you need to borrow the money for a longer period.

It can be worth checking whether you can get an interest-free credit deal from a shop or dealer before you borrow.

Personal loans normally set a fixed rate of interest for the term of your loan. This can help you budget, but if interest rates fall, you could lose out. The longer the period you choose to repay the loan, the lower your monthly repayments, but the more you pay overall. And the larger the amount you borrow, generally speaking, the lower the interest rate.

Watch out for whether there are any early repayment penalties. Lenders can charge you for some of the interest payments they have lost because you have settled the loan before its time. You don't have to take a personal loan from the bank or building society where you have your current account. You can go elsewhere to get a better deal.

Secured loans may be suitable for major expenditures like home improvements. They work like personal loans except that they are secured against your home, and your home is at risk if you default on the payments. On the other hand, they are usually cheaper than personal loans, and if you borrow from your mortgage lender, they can be added to your home loan, giving you longer to repay.

You may have to pay an arrangement fee, and pay to get a valuation on your property.

Credit insurance

Lenders often offer you payment protection insurance to cover your repayments if you lose your job or become ill. It is usually offered as part of a specific loan package, so you can't normally shop around for your own insurance. Look over your loan application form carefully, because some lenders automatically charge you for credit cover unless you tick a box saying you *don't* want it.

As with all types of insurance, go through the small print with a fine-tooth comb. Most credit protection insurance runs out after one or two years only, and may not cover your full repayments. There are often deferral periods of one to three months before the policy comes into operation, so it won't totally shield you from the possibility of running up arrears. And it is unlikely to cover you if you take voluntary redundancy. Costs can be as high as £50 for a £500 loan over one year, so it is worthwhile weighing up whether you really need the cover.

Joint borrowings

If you run your finances jointly with your husband or partner, you may decide to have your borrowings in both your names. It is vital that you are aware of where this leaves you if things go wrong. Under the law, it does not matter who actually spent the money, or whose idea it was to take out the loan — what matters are the terms and conditions of the account.

With credit cards, you cannot have a joint account. The principal account holder can give a card to a secondary holder to use, but he or she remains responsible for all the spending.

If you take out a loan in joint names, you are 'jointly and severally liable' with your husband or partner. That means the lender can enforce the full amount of the debt on both or either of you. It makes no difference if the money was used to buy a new car for your husband or your boyfriend — if you have signed, you can be chased for the full debt.

The same applies to joint current accounts with overdraft facilities — you can be held responsible, whether or not it was you who did the spending. It is not unknown for current accounts to be cleared out totally by one partner.

If you separate from your husband or partner, contact your bank and other lenders straight away. Any account which gives them the facility for more borrowing, for instance a credit card where you are the principal holder or an overdraft facility, should be frozen immediately.

The risks of joint borrowing go much further than just having your current account cleaned out, unfortunately. You can lose your home and be saddled with debts running into tens of thousands of pounds if you take bigger loans jointly with your husband, or if you guarantee loans he has taken out.

Small businessmen often ask their wives to put up the family home as collateral for a loan to back their enterprise. But be very careful before you sign for a loan which puts your home at risk.

Always get independent legal advice first.

Bad references

It is against the law for lenders to discriminate against women when granting credit, either directly or indirectly, for instance by refusing loans to part-time workers, who are mainly female.

There is nothing to stop you applying for credit in your own right — married women do not need their husband's permission.

Most lenders use a system called credit scoring to decide whether or not to grant you a loan. As part of the process, most lenders use information from credit reference agencies.

Contrary to popular myth, credit reference agencies do not keep blacklists. But they do store information from the electoral roll, previous credit accounts and county court judgements for debt.

If you are turned down for credit, you can ask the lender whether they used credit reference agency information, and for the agency's name and address. You can then apply in writing to the agency, enclosing a £1 fee, and ask for any information held about you. If it is incorrect, you can have it put right.

The lender may reconsider your application in the light of incorrect credit reference agency information. But they are not obliged to — lending money is a commercial decision, and you have no right to credit. You also have no right to be told why your application has been refused.

Bad debts incurred by your husband or a partner who lives with you may count against you when you apply for a loan, even if you had nothing to do with the borrowings.

If there is information on your credit reference agency file about people with whom you now have no connection, you should write to the agency and request a notice of disassociation, preventing the agency from giving the information out to lenders.

Dealing with debt

Be honest with yourself if you are running into debt difficulty. Trying to ignore the problem will only make matters worse. Then draw up a plan of campaign. If the situation has not gone too far, you may be able to retrieve it yourself by cutting down on expenses and trying to increase your income.

Draw up a weekly budget and try to identify any areas where you can trim your outgoings. Check whether you may qualify for any benefits, and explore possibilities such as taking in a lodger.

But if that is not enough, inform lenders immediately. Remember that paying your mortgage or rent and fuel bills are priority debts, so concentrate on them first.

Don't be afraid to seek specialist help. Sources of aid include:

- Money advice centres run by local authorities. Look in your telephone directory or ask at the town hall.
- National Debtline, tel: 0121-359 8501.
- Citizen's Advice Bureaux. Look in your telephone book for details of your local CAB.
- If you feel you have fallen victim to a 'loan shark', contact your local trading standards department. Look in the telephone book for their number.

More information

The Office of Fair Trading will deal with complaints if you feel a credit reference agency has treated you unfairly. It also publishes a leaflet, *Debt, A Survival Guide*. Contact:

OFT
PO Box 2
Central Way
Feltham
Middlesex TW14 0TG
Tel: 0171-242 2858

8
Planning a rich retirement

It's easy to put off thinking about your pension — when you're busy working, and perhaps looking after a family too, retirement seems a long way off. But all women should give serious thought to providing for life after work.

The hard fact is that women are still second-class citizens when it comes to retirement. A recent report by leading insurance company Legal & General found women are much more likely than men to suffer unnecessarily from financial pressures once they give up work.

The survey uncovered worrying trends. Because women usually put their families' immediate financial needs first instead of prioritising their own pension, they are placing themselves at a major disadvantage in retirement. Millions of women are in danger of joining an underclass of low income pensioners reliant entirely on the state to support them.

Female workers have several in-built disadvantages in the building up of a good pension. The first is that, because women still on average only earn 79 per cent as much as their male colleagues, they either do not pay or cannot afford to pay as much into a pension.

The second is that most women take career breaks to bring up children or care for elderly relatives — time during which they cannot make contributions to a pension fund. Thirdly, many women work part time, and may not be eligible to join a company pension scheme — only a third of working women are members of an employers' scheme, compared with almost half the male workforce. However, a recent ruling in the European Court of Justice can mean that a woman excluded from a pension scheme as a result of sex discrimination may be able to join and claim pension credits.

In the past, women relied on their husbands to provide. But this option is no longer tenable. One in three marriages end up in the divorce courts, leaving an ex-wife with no automatic right to a share in her former husband's retirement nest-egg. And most women outlive their husbands, in which case they may be forced to eke out an existence on a much reduced widow's pension.

It all sounds deeply gloomy, not to mention unfair. The good news, though, is that all contributions you pay into a pension plan are highly tax-efficient, and by planning ahead and taking responsibility for your own independent pension, you should be able to build yourself a man-sized retirement income.

This chapter and the ones that follow look at pensions from the state, employers and private retirement schemes.

Working women should join a company scheme if they can, and if not, take out a personal pension plan from an insurance company, bank or building society. Full-time wives and mums who do not work outside the home cannot pay into a pension plan, but they should try to build up other savings for retirement. And the earlier you start, the easier — and cheaper — it will be.

Pensions from the State

You are probably entitled to much less from the state than you might imagine. The basic weekly state pension for a single person in 1995/6 is £58.85 or £94.10 for a married couple. Up-to-date rates are listed in leaflet NI196, available from Benefits Agencies.

To qualify for these amounts, however, you must have paid or been credited with National Insurance contributions for roughly nine-tenths of your working life — 44 years for a woman, and 49 years for a man.

Government figures show that in 1992 only 38 per cent of women receiving a state pension were doing so on their own record, not on their husband's. And according to separate figures, in 1991 only 15 per cent of women qualified for a full basic state pension on their own record, compared with nearly 70 per cent of men. Those figures should improve in time, as more women become and remain active in the labour force.

- If you have been employed and paid NI contributions for between a quarter and nine-tenths of your working life, you may be entitled to a reduced state pension.
- Married women who have never worked may be entitled to a pension based on their husband's National Insurance contributions, worth about 60 per cent of what he gets. But you have to wait until your husband reaches 65 before it is paid, and you must be aged 60 or more. If you are under 60, your husband can still claim the extra, but it is called an Adult Dependency Addition. DSS leaflet (A13) NI1 *National Insurance for Married Women* has more detail.
- Many women retiring now have paid a reduced rate of NI contribution, often called the 'married woman's stamp'. This option was withdrawn in 1978, but women who had already taken it were allowed to continue. Unfortunately, reduced rate contributions do not count towards a state pension of your own. If you have never paid anything other than the married woman's stamp you must rely on your husband's contributions for a married couple's pension. You might consider electing to pay full NI contributions now if you are still paying reduced rate.

Home Responsibilities Protection

Women — and men — who have to stay at home to look after children, an elderly relative or a disabled dependant can safeguard their basic state pension rights by claiming Home Responsibilities Protection. If you are not already receiving HRP you can claim at your local Benefits Agency.

State Earnings Related Pension Scheme

The SERPS pension is paid on top of your basic State pension. It is worked out on earnings since 1978 on which you have paid National Insurance contributions. You pay NI contributions on earnings between an upper and a lower weekly limit — in 1995/6 these limits are £58 and £440 respectively. Because of the rising costs of SERPS, the government is downgrading the benefits from the scheme so the most you will receive is falling from a quarter of the average of your best 20 years' earnings to a fifth of the average of your lifetime earnings.

The change to lifetime earnings instead of the best 20 years is particularly damaging to women's prospects of a good SERPS pension, because career breaks caring for children and periods of part-time work will reduce the total average earnings figure. The self-employed are not eligible for a SERPS pension.

Many women are contracted out of SERPS through their company scheme. They are entitled to a guaranteed minimum pension which is roughly the same as what they would have received under SERPS.

A large number of younger women have contracted out through a special personal pension from an insurance company. Contracting out is explained in more detail later in the book.

Equal pension ages

The Government is planning to raise the State pension age for women from 60 to 65, the same as for men, by the year 2020.

Equalisation of pension ages will be phased in over ten years starting in April 2010. Only those born after 6 April 1955 will have to wait right up until 65. Women born before 6 April 1950 will not be affected and will still be able to draw their state pension at age 60. Those born between 1950 and 1955 will have their State pension age delayed for two months for each one month (or part of a month) their birthday falls after 6 April 1950.

So, for instance, if you were born on 14th May 1950, your new state pension age is 60 years 2 months, and you will receive your pension on 6 July 2010.

More information

If you have any questions or worries about your state pension, contact your local Benefits Agency, or ring the Freephone helpline on 0800 666555. The number is 0800 616757 in Northern Ireland, and 0 800 289 011 for Welsh speakers.

For a forecast of your state pension, fill in form BR19 from your local Benefits Agency. If there are gaps in your contribution record, you may be able to make them up by paying extra voluntary contributions now.

9
A pension with your job

It is usually an excellent idea to join a company pension scheme if you can. It's a very tax-efficient way to save. You receive tax relief at your highest rate on all the contributions you make, and your nest-egg grows tax free. You will also benefit from contributions made by your employer.

Company pensions are moving slowly towards equality of the sexes. The good side of this is that more schemes are allowing part-time employees, most of whom are women, to join. The downside is that most schemes have now moved to equal pension ages for men and women, usually 65.

Many people have become worried about the safety of company pension schemes after the late Robert Maxwell was discovered to have plundered millions from company pension funds. The vast majority of schemes, however, are well-run and secure, and the government has produced a Pensions Bill, proposing a series of measures to improve the safety of pension funds. Do not be deterred by the Maxwell scandal — it is highly unlikely to happen to you.

Pension contributions from staff and employers are channelled into a pension fund, which is quite separate from the company you work for. It is run by trustees, who are responsible for managing the fund and making sure pensioners and their families receive the benefits they have been promised.

There are three main types of company pension. It is rare for employees to be offered a choice between schemes — you normally have to take the type your company offers.

Final salary schemes

These are the most common arrangement. Final salary schemes promise to pay a pension based on a proportion of what you are earning on retirement. The proportion depends on how many years you have worked for the company. Most schemes pay a pension of 1/60th or occasionally 1/80th of final salary for every year's service. So if, for instance, Joanna has worked for her company for 20 years, and is a member of a 1/60th scheme, she would receive a pension of 20/60 or one-third of her final salary. The maximum pension you can receive is two-thirds of your final salary. When you finally retire, you are allowed to take part of your pension as a tax-free lump sum. If you work in the public sector or local government, teaching, for example, the pension fraction is 1/80th with a tax-free lump sum in addition.

Company schemes also provide benefits for your dependants if you die. Widowers' pensions are normally a proportion of your pension, whether you die after retiring or in service. If you die in service, your husband and/or family may receive a death benefit, for instance four times your salary.

Typically, you will be asked to contribute around 5 per cent of your salary. Your company will pay in the extra money needed to cover the cost of your benefits.

Money Purchase Schemes

These have become more popular over recent years. Contributions from members and the employer are paid into a fund, often run by an insurance company, which invests the money in stocks, shares, property and government bonds. The pension you will receive is not determined in advance — it depends on the performance of the fund's investments, and on the cost of buying an annuity to provide an income when you retire.

As with a final salary scheme, you can take part of your pension as a tax-free lump sum, and benefits for dependants are often provided.

Hybrid schemes

These are relatively rare, and as their name suggests, they combine the best features of money purchase and final salary schemes. You either receive a pension based on a percentage of your final salary or on the value of the pension fund when you retire, whichever is the greater.

10
Personal pension plans

Women who are unable to join a company pension scheme should consider taking out a personal pension. This works like a money purchase scheme, with your contributions going into an investment pot which is turned into retirement benefits when you stop work.

Personal plans are available from insurance companies, banks and building societies. As with company pensions, any payments you make receive tax relief at your highest rate. So a 25 per cent taxpayer who is an employee would need to pay only £75 to make a contribution worth £100. Self-employed women would pay the full £100 and claim back the tax relief via their tax assessment.

Because of the tax benefits, the Inland Revenue sets limits on the contributions you can make. Women — and men — under 35 can pay up to 17.5 per cent of earnings into a personal pension. For ages 36 to 45, the maximum is 20 per cent; for ages 46 to 50, it is 25 per cent; for ages 51 to 55, it is 30 per cent; for ages 56 to 60 it is 35 per cent and for over 60s it is 40 per cent.

Most employers will not make contributions to a personal pension, and you normally have to pay extra for death benefits and dependants' pensions provided free by company schemes.

However, some employers do contribute to so-called group personal pension plans as an alternative to running a company pension scheme. Frequently they add on death in service benefits at no cost to you.

Choosing a personal pension is not easy, and you may wish to consult an independent financial adviser. He or she should be able to give you more information about the plans, and help you pick one from a reputable company with a good performance record.

You can take out more than one personal pension, which reduces the risk of putting all your money into a poor performer. But that means paying more than one set of start-up charges. With any personal pension, you have to pay set-up charges and an annual management fee, but these can vary from plan to plan. You cannot draw the benefits of a personal pension until you are aged 50.

Lower paid women are at a disadvantage with personal pensions, because if you can only afford small payments, much of your contributions may be eaten up by charges. But if you are an employee, you still receive tax relief on your contributions of at least 25 per cent, even if you do not earn enough to pay tax, or you pay at the lower 20 per cent rate.

There are three main types of personal pension plan. Which you choose depends on how old you are, and how much investment risk you are prepared to take in the hope of earning a bigger pension.

With-profits plans

These are a relatively safe bet. With-profits pensions guarantee you a basic sum on retirement. That guaranteed sum is increased each year as bonuses are added. The bonuses depend on the investment performance of the pension fund you are investing in. Once added, they cannot be taken away. When your plan matures, a final bonus is also added. With-profits plans are suitable for women who do not want to take a big risk with their retirement money.

Unit-linked plans

With a unit-linked plan, your contributions are invested in a fund linked to the stockmarket. The value of the fund rises and falls in line with share values, and what you receive at the end depends on how well it performs. Unit-linked plans are more risky than with-profits, but they offer the chance of far bigger rewards over the long term. They are suitable for younger women, and those prepared to take more risk in the hope of more gain. Normally you will be advised to switch out of a unit-linked plan into with-profits about five years before you are due to retire, so you won't be hit if there is a stock market crash just before you stop work.

Deposit plans

These are the safest option of all. Deposit-based personal pensions are just like bank and building society savings accounts. Your capital is guaranteed not to fall in value, and interest is added at regular intervals. But these are only a good bet if you are either highly opposed to taking any risk, or have five years or less to go to retirement. Over longer periods, they are likely to do much worse than with-profits or unit-linked plans, because inflation eats into the value of your capital.

Contracting out of SERPS

There are also special personal pension plans designed for people who want to contract out of SERPS. The reason you may wish to contract out is that you might achieve better benefits privately than through the state scheme.

You may automatically be contracted out of SERPS through an employer's scheme, or you may choose to contract out yourself.

If you are contracted out through a final salary scheme, you cannot do any worse than with SERPS. If you contract out privately, rather than through a final pay scheme, you could do better than SERPS, or you could do worse.

You contract out privately by opening a specialised personal pension plan from an insurance company. You do not have to pay anything — the money comes from part of your employer's and your National Insurance contributions. These are transferred into your personal pension plan.

You receive tax relief at 25 per cent on your transferred NI contributions and, if you are over 30, a 1 per cent bonus.

Whether or not it makes sense to contract out of SERPS yourself depends mainly on your age and how much you earn. Legal & General advises that it is safer for women who earn less than £7000 to £8000 a year and are aged over 35 to stay in SERPS. Women under 35 on higher earnings should consider contracting out if they are sure they will be working for the next two years and paying contributions into their personal pension.

If you are contracted out, you can contract back in again when you get older or if your earnings drop. You cannot draw your contracted-out SERPS pension until you reach state pension age.

More information

If you have a problem or complaint with a company or personal pension that cannot be resolved to your satisfaction, contact:

The Occupational Pensions Advisory Service
111 Belgrave Road
London SW1V 1RB
Tel: 0171-233 8080

If they cannot resolve the problem, they will pass your complaint to the Pensions Ombudsman.

11
Building a man-sized pension

It's very important for working women to pump up their pensions while they can. There are three good reasons for this: first, most women need to make up for career breaks, second, many women in future will want to retire 'early', before they reach 65; third, because women live longer than men on average, those with a personal pension or money purchase company scheme receive a lower annual pension than a man the same age.

Women who have left pension planning until their late thirties or beyond should make a big effort to boost their pension as soon as possible.

What happens to my pension during a career break?

The most important difference between men and women when it comes to pension planning is that women have to plan to make up for lost time spent looking after the family. Before you can start to plan, though, you need to know your pension rights while you are away from work.

State pension

If you are receiving Statutory Maternity Pay (SMP) you are credited with National Insurance contributions towards your state pension.

Company pension

Most company pension schemes treat time off work to have children whilst you are receiving SMP as pensionable service. Most insist you continue to pay your contributions to the scheme as a percentage of SMP, rather than a percentage of your salary.

If you take more time off after your SMP stops, it is not normally counted for pension benefits. Some schemes may treat you as having left when your SMP stops and rejoining as a new member when you go back to work. That reduces your pension on retirement.

Personal pensions

During any time you are off work and not receiving pay, you cannot make payments to a personal pension plan. Nor will any money be credited to a personal plan to contract out of SERPS, because you are not making any National Insurance contributions. When you go back to work, you can start to pay into your personal pension again. You may wish to do so at a higher rate to make up for lost time.

Full-time wives and mothers

Women who do not carry out any paid work outside the home are not allowed to pay into a pension plan. But it is still important to build up your own independent retirement nest-egg if you can. The chapters on savings and investments earlier in this book give more detail.

Boosting your pension

If you are a member of a company pension scheme you can make additional voluntary contributions (AVCs) to the scheme itself or free standing AVCs (FSAVCs) to an insurance company fund. The most you can pay into a company scheme and AVCs or FSAVCs together is 15 per cent of your total salary each tax year. AVCs of either sort can only be used to boost your pension income, not to enhance the tax-free lump sum the Inland Revenue allows you to take when you retire.

Using additional voluntary contributions to spice up your retirement savings is highly tax-efficient. Like your normal payments into a pension scheme, AVCs and FSAVCs attract tax relief at your highest rate, so a £100 payment would really only cost a basic rate taxpayer £75 and a higher rate taxpayer £60. And once invested, your extra contributions are allowed to grow almost entirely free of gains tax and income tax.

AVCs or FSAVCs?

You can contribute to employers' AVC schemes and an FSAVC plan if you wish, but most people stick to one or the other. AVCs to an employers' scheme very occasionally enable you to purchase 'added years' to make up any shortfall in your pension entitlement. But normally your contributions are invested to produce a fund at retirement which you turn into extra pension.

Before you sign up, check on what benefits the AVCs will provide. As a rule of thumb the charges on AVCs are likely to be lower than on FSAVCs, but you have no control over how the money is invested.

You can buy FSAVCs from insurance companies, banks, building societies, unit trusts, friendly societies and a couple of investment trusts. The charges will probably be higher, but you have a much wider choice of investments.

Personal pensions

Women who have taken out a personal pension plan cannot make AVCs or FSAVCs. But you can increase your retirement fund simply by bumping up your contributions.

You can choose to pay extra to your main plan, or start a new one if you wish.

Early retirement

Many women dream of retiring early, a trend that is likely to grow with the proposed raising of younger women's pension age to 65. A recent survey by insurance company London Life showed only 12 per cent of women had taken any action to make up the shortfall so they would still be able to retire at age 60.

Early retirement is expensive. Not only will you have to wait for your state pension, but you will also get a lower company or personal pension. That's because you have paid in fewer contributions, your pension fund has had less time to grow and your pension provider will have to pay you an income for more years.

So if you do want to retire early, the advice on boosting your pension contributions and other savings as much as you can applies even more.

12
Pension tips for job-changers

Pensions are a highly complex area. Matters are made worse because most company pensions assume people do not change their jobs.

Most women do not work for the same employer throughout their career. If you have a personal pension plan, it is portable, so you can continue to pay in even though you switch jobs.

But if you are a member of a company pension scheme, you must decide what to do with the benefits you have built up. If you have been a scheme member for less than two years, you usually have no choice but to take a refund of your contributions less tax at 20 per cent and often a deduction for National Insurance.

Once you have been a scheme member for two years, you qualify for 'preserved rights'. You can either: leave your pension where it is, switch to a new employer's scheme, or transfer to a personal pension.

Leaving your pension where it is

Your pension rights stay in your former employer's scheme, where they must be increased each year by at least 5 per cent or the rate of inflation, whichever is the lower. When you reach retirement age, you will receive a pension from the scheme.

Moving your pension to a new employer's scheme

You may have the option of transferring your pension rights to your new company's scheme. Your old employer's pension scheme will calculate a 'transfer value' — or cash sum equivalent to the rights you have accumulated. There is no hard and fast formula for working out transfer values, and there has been concern in the pensions industry that some early leavers may get a raw deal. On top of that, your new employer's scheme may place a seemingly low value on your pension rights. But both schemes are supposed to treat you fairly.

Ask for guidance from your new company's pension department.

Transferring your pension to an insurance company

You also have the option of transferring your pension rights to a personal pension plan. This type of transfer has received a great deal of bad publicity recently, after it emerged that many miners, nurses, teachers and other workers had been persuaded by financial advisers and insurance company salespeople to transfer out of their occupational schemes into inferior personal pensions, even though they were not changing jobs. City watchdog the Securities and Investments Board is currently investigating the scandal.

The golden rule is: never transfer out of a company scheme into a personal plan if you are not leaving your job. If you have done so, contact the insurance company or financial adviser where you bought your personal pension. You may also wish to approach your trade union for help.

The Securities and Investments Board is also investigating the scandal of many thousands of job-changers and people made redundant who may have been ill-advised to transfer their rights into personal pensions. The situation here is less clear-cut than that of people who took out a personal plan when they carried on working for the same employer and could have remained a member of the company scheme.

If you are leaving your job, it is only worth transferring to a personal plan if it will provide a better pension in the end. That depends on how well it performs. Insurance companies and advisers have to work out carefully whether transferring is the best advice for you, taking account of the growth needed in the personal plan to match the benefits offered by your company scheme.

It's important to get this decision right — the wrong choice could leave you thousands of pounds out of pocket. So take as much advice as you can. Ask your company scheme for assistance, and consider consulting an independent financial adviser with expertise in the pensions field. There is no hurry to make up your mind — you can transfer your pension rights out of an old scheme at any time.

More information

If you have benefits in old company schemes that you cannot trace, consult:

The Registrar of Pension Schemes
Occupational Pensions Board
PO Box 1NN
Newcastle upon Tyne NE99 1NN
Tel: 0191-225 6393

13
Pensions and partners

Although it is imperative for women to build up their own independent pension, those who are in a marriage or partnership need to do so in tandem with their partner's plans.

It is wise to take a close interest in your husband or partner's pension arrangements — not just in case you divorce, but also to identify any gaps in your joint planning. Is his pension large enough, for example, or is he relying on a contribution from you?

You should also find out what his company or private pension would pay to you and your children if he died before retirement, and fill any gaps in your life assurance as appropriate.

Those who are living together should check whether it makes a difference that they are not actually married.

Pensions and divorce

What happens to pensions when a couple divorces is one of the biggest issues troubling the financial world at the moment. The husband's pension is often a couple's biggest asset after the family home.

But if you divorce, you have no automatic right to a share in it from your husband's company or private scheme, even if you did not get a chance to build up your own pension because you were caring for home and family.

If your husband remarries, his new wife will take over any pension benefits you had. The government is being lobbied at top level to change this unfair situation, but as yet, nothing has changed.

Pensions must be negotiated as part of a divorce settlement. Valuing your husband's pension rights and your share is highly complex and outside the scope of most solicitors. Although it is expensive, it could be worth taking advice from a pensions specialist.

Courts can — and in Scotland must — take pension rights into account when coming to an agreement on how the assets are split. The structure of most pension schemes makes it impossible to divide up the pension rights themselves, so the courts normally rule that the wife must be given a larger share of the other assets in compensation.

If you divorce and do not remarry before state pension age, you can qualify for a basic state pension based on your own and your ex-husband's National Insurance contributions. You can also claim a state pension on your ex-husband's record if you split up after state pension age.

More information

If you need financial advice, consult an adviser authorised by the the Personal Investment Authority (PIA). Some advisers are independent, and can give guidance on all the products in the market-place. Others are tied to one company, and can only advise on its products. Make sure you know which type of adviser you are dealing with.

You can obtain specialist pensions advice from a member of:

The Society of Pension Consultants
Ludgate House
Ludgate Circus
London EC4A 2AB
Tel: 0171-353 1688

or:

The Association of Consulting Actuaries
1 Wardrobe Place
London EC4V 5AH
Tel: 0171-248 3163

National & Provincial Building Society Financial Services for Women produces a useful *Pensions Guide for Women*, available free, tel: 0800 600200.

Fair Shares is a pressure group campaigning for fair division of pensions on divorce:

Fair Shares
14 Park Road
Rugby
Warwickshire CV21 2QH

14
Living together

The number of couples living together has increased sharply in the past 20 years. In 1972, just 16 per cent of women lived with their future husband before marriage. Now, according to official statistics, the proportion is 62 per cent.

At the same time, the number of marriages has fallen by more than 10 per cent in the past ten years, because more couples are choosing to live together as a long-term alternative to marriage. The stigma of having a baby outside marriage is now fast disappearing. Nearly a third of all babies are born to unmarried mothers — of those, more than half are born to couples who live together.

But despite the increasing popularity of living together, both the law and the tax system give women who cohabit fewer rights than their married counterparts. Contrary to popular myth, you do not automatically gain similar rights to a married woman after you have lived with your boyfriend for a certain length of time.

Common law marriage has not existed in this country for more than 200 years, and in fact you have no automatic entitlement to a share in your partner's property or to widow's benefits, no matter how long you have been together or how many of his children you have had.

So if you are living with your partner, whether as a prelude to marriage or as a permanent arrangement, you need to be aware of the financial implications. Most of the potential problems can be avoided if you and your partner agree on what you want to happen financially if you split up or one of you dies, and then seeing a solicitor to draw up legal agreements and wills.

Your home

Moving in with a partner is a serious financial step. Women who are not married to their partner need to consider the following points very carefully:

- *Do you have any rights to the home?* If you move into a home your boyfriend owns in his sole name, you have no claim on it if your relationship breaks down. Whether you contributed towards the mortgage or expenses is irrelevant. The same applies if you move into rented accommodation that is in his name alone.

    But equally, if he moves into a home you are buying in your own name, he has no rights over it.

- *Who owns the property?* When you buy a home jointly with your partner, there are two different ways to own the property: joint tenancies and tenancies in common. If you are joint tenants and the other partner dies, their half of the house automatically passes to the other person. But if you are tenants in common, the deceased's share will go to their next of kin — which will not be their partner unless they specify so in a will. Tenants in common normally own a half share in the property, but ownership can be split in any other proportion, for instance 70 : 30 if one of you contributed much more to buying the property than the other.

- *Should we take out a joint endowment?* There's no need to. You can help make things easier if you do split up by each arranging a separate endowment or PEP in your own name to cover your half of the mortgage.

- *What happens if you split up?* If you want to remain in the home, your partner must agree to be taken off the mortgage deeds. You will then have to buy him out, and you will become responsible for the full mortgage.

    You will need to seek permission from your bank or

building society to have your partner's name taken off the deeds. They are entitled to refuse if they believe you will not be capable of meeting the mortgage instalments alone.
- *What happens if my partner absconds leaving me to pay the full mortgage?* Sadly, the most common cause of repossession is breakdown in relationships. When you take out a joint mortgage, both of you are jointly and severally liable for the full amount — so if your partner can't or won't pay, the lender can pursue you for the whole instalments.

  Keep your lender informed of any difficulties, and try to come to an arrangement where you carry on making payments of as much as you can afford. That way they are more likely to be sympathetic and less likely to repossess.
- *What is your tax position?* Unmarried couples can claim MIRAS — Mortgage Interest Relief at Source — on the interest on the first £30,000 of their home loan. Relief is granted at 15 per cent in the 1995/6 tax year. If you took out your mortgage before August 1988, you each receive MIRAS on £30,000. But if you marry or take out a new mortgage, you will only receive one lot of tax relief.

Making a will

If your partner has not made a will, you will inherit *nothing*. Everything he owns, including his share of your joint home, could go to his next of kin, whether that be children, parents, brothers and sisters — or even a separated wife to whom he is still legally married. If he has no next of kin, the government can claim the estate.

- Both partners should make a will to avoid such problems occurring. It is especially important to do so if you have children. A will also lets you appoint legal guardians for young children in case anything happens to you.
- Women whose live-in partner dies without making a will can make a claim on some of his estate under the Inheritance (Provision for Family and Dependants) Act 1975. But this is

complicated and expensive. Even if your claim is successful — which is far from guaranteed — it could be years before you see any money and your legal bills are likely to be high.
- Unmarried partners do not enjoy the same exemptions from inheritance tax as married women. Anything a husband or wife leaves to his or her spouse is free of inheritance tax. But if your unmarried partner leaves his estate to you, tax at 40 per cent is charged on anything over £154,000 (the nil rate band in the 1995/6 tax year. One way to avoid the tax is by taking out a life assurance policy. This is explained in more detail later in the chapter.
- If you marry later, you will both need to change your wills as the old ones become invalid.

Insurance

Life insurance should be a priority for anyone with dependants. Partners living together both need to take out an adequate amount of life cover, especially if you have children. Unmarried couples can take out a joint life assurance policy, which will pay out when the first partner dies. This is cheaper than taking out two single policies, but the surviving partner will no longer be insured after the policy has paid out, which is a problem if you are left with dependent children.

Taking out a joint policy can lead to problems when a couple splits up.

Alternatively, you can take out a single life policy written in trust for your partner. If you die, the money is paid direct to them, and is not classed as part of your estate. You can write a policy specifically intended to pay an expected inheritance tax bill if you wish. When both partners take out single life policies, the surviving partner will continue to be insured if the other dies, which is important if you have children.

Tax and benefits

The tax authorities treat unmarried couples as two single people. You both receive a single personal allowance of £3525 in the

1994/5 tax year. You will not get the Married Couples' Allowance, currently £1720.

Unmarried women with dependent children are entitled to the Additional Personal Allowance, also £1720. In the 1995/6 tax year, relief is granted at 15 per cent, so the the value of the allowance is £258.

Although you are treated as single people when it comes to receiving tax allowances, the DSS often treats cohabiters as man and wife when you claim benefits. Both your incomes are taken into account when assessing your entitlement to means tested benefits such as Income Support and Housing Benefit. But for other benefits, such as Unemployment Benefit, your partner's income is not taken into account.

Unmarried partners are not entitled to widow's benefits from the state.

Savings

You can set up joint savings accounts so the signature of both of you is needed to withdraw money, or so either one of you can sign. The same applies to bank accounts. Many unmarried couples keep separate accounts for individual use, and a joint one for bills. Both partners are equally liable for any debts run up on a joint account, regardless of which partner actually spent the money. You can specify that a joint account must not have an overdraft facility if you wish.

Pensions

It is unwise even for married women to rely on their husband's pension. Unmarried women should make even more effort to build up their own provision. Unlike married women, who may be able to claim up to half of their husband's company pension if he dies, you normally have no entitlement. See Chapters 9 to 13 for more detail on pension planning.

More information

The Co-operative Bank has published a free booklet, *Living Together: A Guide for Women Co-habiters*, tel: 0171-637 4890.

Independent financial advisers Fiona Price & Partners publish a factsheet, *Living Together*, available free from:

Fiona Price & Partners
33 Great Queen Street
Covent Garden
London WC2B 5AA
Tel: 0171-430 0366

The Consumers' Association publishes a helpful book, *Wills and Probate* and a *Make Your Will* action pack, available from the Which? Bookshop, 359–61 Euston Road, London NW1, or tel: 0800 252100.

15
Money and marriage

When you are in the throes of true love, it probably seems deeply unromantic to think about money. But no couple can escape the realities of having to deal with cash.

And whilst no one marries in the expectation they will get a divorce, it is possible to arrange your finances in such a way that the economic damage is minimised if you do split up. According to independent financial adviser Fiona Price, who specialises in dealing with women, the most important thing for couples to do is to talk about money from the start.

Both should be aware of the other's debts and assets before marriage to avoid potential pitfalls and to maximise your joint finances. How much privacy and independence you want is obviously an individual issue, and each couple can come to their own arrangements. But it is always better that these are discussed fully and agreed on.

Money, lack of it and attitudes to it are one of the major sources of rows between couples and can even be the cause of marital breakdown. If one of you is a spendthrift and the other is a skinflint, it is obviously going to be a problem area.

Fiona Price recommends couples to take an independent but complementary approach to joint financial planning. That way, you both have your own savings, pension and bank accounts under your sole control, which puts you in a better situation if things do go wrong. But it also allows you to plan in such a way that you can make the most of your joint assets.

Relying on your husband financially is nothing less than foolhardy. It leaves you extremely vulnerable in the event of a divorce or if you are widowed. Marriage will always entail giving up some financial independence. But the good news is that the bad old days when women had to get their husband's permission to take out a loan and were treated as his chattel in the eyes of the tax authorities are now over.

Preparing for the big day

Couples should start to think about financial planning well before they marry. The average cost of a wedding is now nearly £8000, so unless you have very generous parents or want a minimum of fuss and show, you'll need to start saving well in advance.

You'll also have all the costs of setting up a new home and kitting it out. Beware of taking on too much credit at this stage — it's better to make do with second-hand furniture and wait until you've saved for what you want than ending up deep in debt.

Any marriage involves big financial changes. Young couples might be moving away from their parents' home and having to learn to budget for the first time.

But more established career women who delay marriage until their thirties may have built up fairly substantial assets in their own right and, for instance, have a flat to sell before moving into the marital home.

Pre-nuptial agreements laying down how a couple's property and assets would be split in the event of divorce are common in the United States. They strike most British people as distasteful, however, and in any case are not binding in English law.

Tax and marriage

The tax advantages of marriage are not as great as they once were, but wedding bells do still bring some tax perks:

- Since the 1990/1 tax year, women have been treated as independent people in the eyes of the tax authorities, instead of just a chattel of their husband. It means you will enjoy privacy over your tax affairs — but the downside is you are responsible for filling in your own tax return.

- Husband and wife are each taxed on their own income and capital gains, and each have their own tax-free Personal Allowance, £3525 in the 1995/6 tax year.
- When you marry you become entitled to the Married Couples' Allowance of £1720 in the 1995/6 tax year. Relief on the allowance is granted at 15 per cent in 1995/6, so its value is £258.
- The allowance automatically goes to the husband. But the wife can claim half without his permission. If both partners agree, the wife can have the full allowance, provided you tell the tax authorities before the end of the previous tax year.
- In the year of marriage, the allowance is reduced by 1/12 for each month after the end of the tax year you are still single. So if you marry on 14 May 1995, you will receive 11/12 of the allowance in the 1995/6 tax year.
- The tax authorities allow relatives to give you cash wedding presents free of inheritance tax. Each parent of the bride or groom can give up to £5000 tax free, grandparents can give £2500 and anyone else can give you £1000.

Joint savings and investments

It makes sense for married couples to have savings and investments in their own name, not just to give them independence, but to make the most of tax breaks:

- Husband and wife each have their own tax-free allowance for Personal Equity Plans, TESSAs and National Savings. It makes sense for you both to make use of the tax shelters.
- Any profits you make on shares or other assets are subject to capital gains tax. But husbands and wives each have their own annual tax-free allowance, £6000 in the 1995/6 tax year. So if one of you will exceed the tax-free threshold, you can save tax by transferring assets to your partner. Gifts of assets between man and wife are free of capital gains tax — but gifts to anyone else may incur a tax charge.

- If one partner earns less than the other and pays tax at a lower rate, it makes sense to transfer investments into their name. That way, the interest or dividends will be taxed at a lower rate. But any gifts of this sort must be outright, with no strings attached.

Making a will

Any will you made while you were still single becomes invalid when you marry, so you will need to make a new one. If you or your husband have not yet made a will, you must both do so as soon as possible.

Clearly, this is a sensitive subject, and many people irrationally feel the very thought of making a will is 'tempting fate'. But if your husband does not make a proper will, you will be left in a very vulnerable situation.

Wives do not automatically inherit everything when their husband dies, in spite of persistent myths to that effect.

If there is no will and you have children, the widow gets the first £125,000 of the estate, and a life interest in half the rest. A life interest means you can draw interest or use possessions, but you cannot sell anything or draw on capital. The other remaining half goes to the children, who also inherit the capital bearing the life interest when the widow dies.

If there are no children, the widow gets the first £200,000 of the estate, and half the remainder. The remaining half is shared between other relatives.

This may sound like a lot of money and not relevant to you. But many people underestimate the value of their estate, especially when you add in the family home.

Making a tax-efficient will can also help minimise or avoid inheritance tax, which is payable on estates worth more than £154,000. You can draw up a will so that husband and wife both make use of their own £154,000 allowance.

Life cover is a must

Both of you should have adequate life cover, to make sure the other will not be thrown into financial hardship if anything happens. State benefits for widows are not generous — the widowed mother's allowance, for instance, most likely to be claimed by younger women with children, is paid at a full rate of £58.85 in 1995/6.

Young fathers suddenly left with children to support are even worse off — there are no state benefits especially for widowers.

More information

Independent financial advisers Fiona Price & Partners publishes a factsheet on money and marriage, available free from:

Fiona Price & Partners
33 Great Queen Street
Covent Garden
London WC2B 5AA
Tel: 0171-430 0366

The Inland Revenue publishes some useful leaflets, available in tax offices: IR80, *Income Tax and Married Couples*, and IR110, *A Guide for People with Savings*.

The Consumers' Association publishes a helpful book, *Wills and Probate*, and a *Make Your Will* action pack, available from the Which? Bookshop, 359–61 Euston Road, London NW1, or tel: 0800 252100.

16
Financial family planning

Few couples appreciate the true price of parenthood before their children arrive. It may be just as well, for according to a survey by *Moneywise* magazine, the total cost of bringing up a child for the first 16 years could come to a massive £250,000 in a traditional family where the mother gives up work and stays at home until the child is a teenager. That doesn't include expensive 'extras' such as a nanny, private school fees or higher education.

Clearly, this points to a need for financial planning, preferably before your baby is born.

First steps

When your baby is born you will need to budget for clothes, prams and equipment, and perhaps much larger expenses if you want to move to a bigger house, say, or extend your present home. If you decide to take a break from work, you may also want to build up your own independent savings. So even if you don't have any immediate plans to start a family, it is worth saving for the future.

If you have five or more years to go before you plan to have children, you have time to save a tidy sum. Tax-free options include a TESSA, where you can save up to £9000 over five years, and National Savings certificates. See Chapters 2 and 3 for more details.

Women who want to have children in the future should also try to pay extra into their pension plan while they can to make up for the time they will lose whilst bringing up a family. See Chapter 11 for more information.

Of course, most young couples do not map out their lives so far ahead, and often cannot afford to set aside large sums while they are also meeting the costs of setting up a first home. But it is still possible to do some forward planning.

Many prospective parents want to move to a larger home before they start a family. It may be sensible to take out a fixed rate mortgage covering the first two to five years, so that you are sure what your repayments will be and you are protected from interest rate rises.

Protecting your family

Life insurance is an absolute necessity for couples intending to have children. You will need higher cover in the early years, and less when the children are grown up and no longer dependent on you. Wives — or husbands — who stay at home to care for the kids still need insurance.

All parents should make a will. If you do not, your family can be left in financial chaos, and your money might not go to the people you wished. A will also allows you to name a guardian for your child in case anything happens to you.

Benefits for mothers

Child Benefit is paid to all mothers at £10.40 per week in 1995/6 for the first child and £8.45 a week for each other child under 16 (or under 19 if they are still in full-time education). Single parents can also claim One Parent Benefit, paid at a single rate of £6.30 per week regardless of how many children you have.

In addition, pregnant women are entitled to free maternity care, free dental care, free parenthood preparation classes and free prescriptions. After the birth you are entitled to free dental care and prescriptions.

School fees

Proud parents who are ambitious to send their children to Eton or Cheltenham Ladies College — or even a modest private school — need to plan particularly carefully. It is not just the wealthy who want to give their children the advantage of a private education. But sending your child to a day school can cost between £3000 and £8000 a year, rising to £6000 to £12,000 for boarders.

Your options for school fees planning depend on your timescale, your tax position, and how much risk you are prepared to take.

The basic ways of paying are:

- Pay the fees as you go out of your income.
- Take out a loan or second mortgage to pay.
- Invest a lump sum or make regular savings in advance.

Option three is the ideal one — it will make the whole process less painful, and will cost you less.

If you have more than five years to plan ahead for school fees, your investment choices include educational trusts, specialist school fee plans or tax-free Personal Equity Plans.

In the medium term, if you have five years or less to go, consider tax-free TESSAs, savings accounts and deposit accounts.

Saving for children

Parents and grandparents are often keen to give their children a good start in life by setting up savings accounts for them. Provided your child's income does not exceed his or her personal allowance of £3525 in the 1995–6 tax year, any savings income is tax-free. Make sure you register your child as a non-taxpayer using form R85, available from banks and building societies, and he or she will receive her savings interest with no tax deducted.

But there are controls on the amount of money parents can put into savings accounts in a child's name, designed to avoid tax evasion. If more than £100 is earned on money that came from either parent in any one tax year, it will be taxed. Each parent has their own £100 limit, so the child can earn up to £200 if mum and dad both make gifts.

If the money comes from grandparents, however, the clause does not apply. Grandparents can also cut down potential inheritance tax bills by making gifts to children during their lifetimes. They can give up to £3000 each tax year free of tax, along with an unlimited number of gifts up to £250.

National Savings Children's Bonus Bonds are a good home for up to £1000 of savings – the interest is tax-free. Accounts are designed to run for five years.

If you can commit yourself to saving on behalf of a child or grandchild for ten years, a friendly society Baby Bond could be a good option. The maximum investment is £25 per month or £270 a year, and many schemes offer 'half plans'. The bonds are linked to the stock market and the payout is tax-free. But if you cash in before ten years, you may get very little back. See Chapters 2 and 3 for more detail.

More information

The Independent Schools Information Service publishes a guide to independent schools and a range of booklets covering ways to fund school fees and information on scholarships and grants:

ISIS
56 Buckingham Gate
London SW1E 6AE
Tel: 0171-630 8793

17
Your maternity rights

The decision to have a baby brings many new considerations for working women. Whether you want to return to work full or part time, work at home or devote yourself to motherhood depends on individual preference and on what you can afford.

But it makes sense to know your rights at work, and to discuss the alternatives — and their financial consequences — fully with your partner or family.

Maternity rights for working women

New rules came into effect during 1994 giving pregnant women improved legal rights at work, along with new maternity benefit rules. Some of the most important aspects of the new rules, which apply to women in England, Scotland and Wales are described below. The position in Northern Ireland is similar but not exactly the same.

While you are pregnant

- Whether you work full or part time, you are entitled to reasonable time off for ante-natal care, with pay. This can include not only medical examinations but also relaxation and parentcraft classes.
- It is against the law for an employer to dismiss a woman or select her for redundancy purely or mainly because she is pregnant or has given birth.
- If you are dismissed during pregnancy or maternity leave you are entitled to a written statement of the reasons.

Time off to have a baby

- All pregnant employees are entitled to at least fourteen weeks statutory maternity leave, regardless of their length of service or hours of work.
- During that period, you are entitled to all the benefits of your contract, such as holiday rights and payments by your employer into a company pension scheme. You are not automatically entitled to receive pay, though you may qualify for Statutory Maternity Pay.
- If you have worked for the same employer full time (at least 16 hours a week) for at least two continuous years, you are also entitled to an additional period of maternity absence on top of your maternity leave.
- Maternity absence lasts from the end of your maternity leave until the 28th week after your baby is born. Part-timers must have worked at least 8 hours a week for five continuous years to qualify for maternity absence. The period of continuous employment is calculated up to the eleventh week before your baby is due. Your employer must keep your job open for you if you wish to return.

Maternity benefits

There are two main benefits pregnant women can claim: Statutory Maternity Pay and Maternity Allowance.

- Your employer must pay SMP if you have worked for them continuously for 26 weeks up to and including the fifteenth week before you expect your baby to be born. Your average earnings for the eight weeks up to and including the fifteenth week before the expected birth must have been at least £59 a week.
- If you fulfil those conditions, you are entitled to at least 18 weeks' SMP, whether or not you intend to return to work. SMP is only payable while you are absent from work, but you can carry on working right up until the birth and still keep your 18 week entitlement.

- For the first six weeks you will receive SMP at 90 per cent of your average weekly earnings, with a minimum payment of £52.50. It is paid in the same way and at the same time as your normal earnings. During the remaining 12 weeks, you will receive a flat SMP payment of £52.50. All the rates quoted apply to 1995/6.
- If you are not entitled to SMP, your employer must fill in DSS form SMP1, and give it to you, to help you claim Maternity Allowance.
- Women who do not qualify for SMP but have paid National Insurance contributions in 26 out of the 66 weeks ending with the week before they expect their baby to arrive are entitled to claim a maximum of 18 weeks' Maternity Allowance if:
  - either they are employed but do not qualify for SMP; or
  - they have recently been employed; or
  - they are self-employed.
- You can claim on form MA1, available from Benefits Agencies or ante-natal clinics. Maternity Allowance is only payable when you are not at work. It is usually paid by order book, which can be cashed each week at a post office of your choice.
- You receive a sum of £52.50 a week if you were employed during the fifteenth week before your baby is due, or £45.55 if you were not employed or you were self-employed. These rates are for 1995/6.
- If you are not entitled to SMP or Maternity Allowance, you may still be able to claim Income Support. For more information, see DSS leaflet IS1, *Income Support*.

What you must tell your employer — and when

If you want to claim maternity leave and SMP, you must tell your employer you are pregnant, and when you expect the baby to be born. Normally, you will need a medical certificate as confirmation. If you want to go back to work after a period of maternity absence, you should mention this at the same time.

You should also tell your employer when you intend to start your maternity leave and when you want to receive SMP. You must make both these notifications at least 21 days before you intend to start taking maternity leave.

If you want to go back to work immediately after the end of your maternity leave, you do not have to give advance notice to your employer.

But if you want to return before then, you should give your employer seven days' notice of your date of return. Women who take maternity absence as well (see above) must give 21 days notice of their date of return. Your employer may send you a written request to confirm you intend to return to work. The earliest they can write is 21 days before the end of your maternity leave. If you do not reply within 14 days, you lose the right to return.

More information:

The Employment Department publishes some useful booklets:

PL 710, *Employment Rights for Expectant Mothers* and PL958, *Maternity Benefits: A Guide for Employers and Employees*, both available from Job Centres.

The Department of Social Security also has two useful booklets: NI 17A, *A Guide to Maternity Benefits*, and FB8, *Babies and Benefit*, available from Benefits Agencies, some post offices and public libraries.

18
Combining work and home

More and more women return to work after having a baby, either to fulfil their career ambitions or simply to make ends meet. But for most the decision is not an easy one. You and your husband or partner need to work out the most suitable solution in terms of hours and working arrangements. But whatever you decide, there will be repercussions for your finances.

It is worth carrying out a basic cost/benefit analysis to help work out the financial consequences of your decision. On the benefit side are the wages or salary you will earn. On the cost side you need to list the expenses of childcare.

The government has introduced measures to help lower income families with children get back into the workforce. From October 1994, people on Family Credit can receive a maximum of £28 extra benefit a week towards the cost of a registered childminder, day nursery or other arrangement to care for a child under the age of 11.

Even so, after knocking off the expense of a childminder or nanny, it may not look worthwhile returning to work purely on financial grounds. But you also need to think about the 'sanity factor' — whether you need to get out of the house — and the longer-term implications. If you carry on working you may be able to command salary increases or promotions in future, whereas if you take a break until your children are older, you may have to return to work at a lower level.

Find out what your employer offers. If you return to work immediately after your statutory maternity leave or absence, you are entitled to come back to the same job, with the same terms and conditions. But some companies allow you to take longer breaks of several years after which you can return to a job of equal status. Usually you will be expected to do several weeks' work a year to keep in touch.

Part-time work

Many women opt to return to work part time after the birth of a baby, or seek out flexible working arrangements.

About one in four of all employees in Britain is a part-timer, and more than four out of five of these are women.

For the purposes of employment rights, part time means working between eight and 16 hours a week. Under the 'hours rule' part-timers doing less than 16 hours a week traditionally had to work for five years to win the right to bring an unfair dismissal claim or receive statutory redundancy pay, whilst full-timers only need two years' service.

They were also often excluded from company pension schemes. A recent case in the House of Lords decided that the 'hours rule' was discriminatory and part-timers should have the same rights as full-timers after two years' service. But the government has not yet amended the law.

Part-timers should not be denied membership to the company pension scheme simply because of the fact they work fewer hours.

Many part-timers get pro-rata holidays, sometimes including bank holidays. Whether or not you receive other benefits such as staff discounts, cheap mortgages or season ticket loans varies from company to company.

Flexible working

In addition to straightforward part-time work, your employer may offer you flexible working options such as job-sharing, flexitime and term-time working.

Job-sharing is where you share one full-time job with another worker. This is often a sensible solution — but you need a good relationship with your co-worker for it to succeed. If your employer operates a flexitime scheme, you can choose the times at which you start and stop work, within limits.

Some employers also operate annual hours schemes, where you contract to work a certain number of hours each year, but have some flexibility over when you do them.

If your employer does not have any formal schemes for flexible working, you may be able to negotiate a deal.

Working from home

Modern technology means many jobs can now be done from home with the aid of a telephone and a computer terminal. It can allow women to tailor their work to the needs of their family, and means big savings in both time and money on travel. But you will still need to make childcare arrangements if you have children under school age.

Some companies, including BT and computer giant ICL, allow selected employees to work from home. Alternatively, you may join the ranks of self-employed people who run a business from home. But beware of exploitative schemes. A recent report by the National Group on Homeworking found up to a million homeworkers, mainly women, earned an average of £1.28 an hour, with some working for as little as 30p an hour.

If you are self-employed and working at home, there are a number of financial factors to consider:

- You may be eligible for tax relief on a proportion of your heating, lighting, cleaning and insurance bills.
- If you use part of your home solely for business, you may be liable for capital gains tax on any profits you make on that part if you sell your home
- If you use part of your home for business purposes without telling your insurance company, it could invalidate your home insurance policy.

More information

The Women Returners' Network aims to help women get back to work or gain new qualifications:
The Women Returners' Network
8 John Adam Street
London WC2N 6EZ
Tel: 0171-839 8188

The WRN publishes a useful book, *Returning to Work, A Directory of Education and Training for Women*, available in good public libraries or from:

MJ Publishing
Garden Cottage
Youngsbury
Ware
Herts SG12 OTZ
Price £15.50 (including postage and packing).

Parents at Work is a charity providing practical information on childcare and on companies operating family-friendly employment policies. It publishes a very useful book, *Balancing Work and Home*, available from:

Parents at Work
77 Holloway Road
London N7 8JZ
Tel: 0171-700 5771
Price £5.50 (including postage and packing).

Educational charity New Ways to Work provides free advice and information for people who would like to work flexibly. Contact NWW at:

New Ways to Work
309 Upper Street
London N1 2TY
Tel: 0171-226 4026

The Employment Department publishes a useful booklet: *Be Flexible: A Guide to Flexible Working*, available from:

Cambertown Ltd
Unit 8
Commercial Road
Goldthorpe
Rotherham
South Yorks
S63 9BL
Tel: 01709 888688

Independent financial advisers Fiona Price & Partners publishes a factsheet, *Planning a Career Break and a Return to Work*, available free from:

Fiona Price & Partners
33 Great Queen Street
Covent Garden
London WC2B 5AA
Tel: 0171-430 0366

The Consumers' Association publishes an excellent book, the *Which ? Guide to Earning Money At Home*, available from the Which? Bookshop, 359–61 Euston Road, London NW1, or tel: 0800 252100.

The Financial Forum for Women publishes two factsheets, *Being at Home and Part-time Work*, available on 0800 590682.

19
Women mean business

According to Barclays Bank, almost a quarter of self-employed people are women, a 78 per cent increase on ten years ago. And research by NatWest bank shows that 27 per cent of new business start-ups are now run by female entrepreneurs.

Although most women will not end up running a multi-million pound international empire like Anita Roddick's small business which ended up as the Body Shop, research shows their businesses may have a better chance of success because they are more inclined than men to seek training.

Self-employment can offer women with families more flexibility over when they work. But since the average self-employed person works 75 hours a week, it doesn't mean you will have more time to spend with family and friends.

Your business plan

All would-be business women should draw up a business plan as a first step. This is essential for when you approach your bank or another backer for finance, and will also help clarify all aspects of the idea in your own mind. Don't just view the business plan as a number-crunching exercise to keep the bank manager happy. It should cover all aspects of the business and you should review it at regular intervals after starting up to see how far you are achieving your aims. It should include:

- A brief description of your business.
- Details of your target market, your main competitors, and why you think you can succeed.
- What the unique selling point is of the business.
- Your CV, detailing your past experience and qualifications,

stressing those relevant to the new business. If you have a business partner, include their CV as well.
- Details of how you intend to price your product or service, and how you have arrived at the figure.
- How you see the business developing in the future.
- A cash flow forecast, showing the money you expect to come in and go out and a profit forecast. Detail how you arrive at the figures. This will show how likely the proposition is to succeed. Banks will normally provide you with forms for this.
- The amount of capital you are putting into the business.
- The amount of money you need to raise in addition to get the business off the ground, and details of any security you can offer, eg your home, and how you intend to repay.
- Details of any other sources of finance, eg loans from family.

Banks are the main source of finance for small businesses. If you take out a business loan, you are normally expected to offer security, for instance your home or a life assurance policy. If you are a married woman, your bank may ask your husband to guarantee the loan. If you are using a jointly owned home as security for a business loan, your husband should get independent financial advice before signing any guarantees. You may also be eligible for loans and grants.

Tax, VAT and financial planning

You must inform the Inland Revenue that you have started up a business, and fill in form 41G. Also tell the Department of Social Security and fill in form CF11 giving details of your business and your National Insurance number. It's worth employing an accountant to help with your tax affairs. Self-employed people pay tax on the profit they have made, less various business expenses.

If your profits are more than £3310 in the 1995/6 tax year, you have to pay Class 2 National Insurance contributions at a rate of £5.85 a week. And if your profits are more than £6640, you must pay Class 4 National Insurance contributions at 7.3 per cent of your profit over £6640 up to £22,880. DSS leaflet FB30, *Self-Employed? A Guide to Your NI Contributions and Social Security Benefits*, gives more information.

If the turnover of your business is more than £46,000 in the 1995/6 tax year, you must also register for VAT. You can opt to do so if you have a lower turnover — in some cases this can be advantageous. VAT leaflet VAT700/1, *Should I be registered for VAT?* gives more information.

Women starting their own business also need to take care of some other important aspects of financial planning. You should have life cover to take care of any business debts in case anything happens to you. A pension plan is a priority, and also consider permanent health insurance in case you fall ill for a long period.

More information

Inland Revenue leaflets IR 28, *Starting in Business*, IR 57, *Thinking of Working for Yourself*, IR 104, *Simple Tax Accounts*, and IR 105, *How your Profits are Taxed*, are all useful.

The 1995 edition of the *Lloyds Bank Small Business Guide* by Sara Williams is an invaluable handbook. It is published by Penguin and is available in bookshops price £15.00.

The Women's Enterprise Forum aims to help female entrepreneurs. Write to:

The Women's Enterprise Forum
c/o Sandra Brusby
Warrington Business Venture
Warrington Business Park
Long Lane
Warrington
Cheshire WA22 8TX
Tel: 01925 633309

NatWest bank has produced a publication, *The Business Start-up Guide*, including specimen business plans, cashflow and profit forecasts, available free from any branch. The bank also produces a *Small Business Information Directory* which details the help available locally to small businesses, such as local grants, support groups and export initiatives. It is free and locally tailored by postcode.

20
Dealing with divorce

All too many women are forced to deal with the financial consequences of divorce and of being a single parent.

Divorce is at historically high levels. For every hundred marriages in the early 1990s, there are now 58 divorces. It seems to be a popular male belief that women use divorce as an excuse to take their ex-husband to the cleaners. But the truth is women are far more likely to suffer financially as a consequence of marital breakdown, especially if they are left with young children. Government figures show that nine out of ten lone parents, of whom more than half are divorced women, are dependent on state benefits to survive.

If you have just decided to divorce or separate, it is an emotionally traumatic time. Often, money can become yet another battleground for a sparring couple, and negotiating a fair financial settlement can be extremely stressful. For some women, who have always left the family finances to their husband, there is the additional stress of having to make money decisions for the first time.

A Financial Settlement

Your basic aim is to negotiate a fair financial settlement for yourself and your children. At this stage, your husband's solicitor may ask you for a statement of your income and outgoings. It makes sense to take stock in any case, so you can realistically appraise the situation, and perhaps identify any ways of improving it, such as cutting down on expenses.

You will be entitled to a proportion, not necessarily half, of your joint assets. The most important of these, in most cases, are the family home and the man's pension rights.

There are no hard and fast rules over what share of the assets you should have, or on the level of maintenance for yourself, though maintenance for your children is covered by the Child Support Act.

Find a good solicitor who specialises in divorce to help you. Remember you may be entitled to Legal Aid — leaflets are available from your solicitor or your local Citizen's Advice Bureau, or from the Legal Aid Board.

You do not have to accept the first offer your ex-spouse makes. But try to be realistic. And remember that the bad behaviour of either partner is very rarely taken into account when deciding on financial settlements. Apart from highly exceptional cases, a court would consider it irrelevant.

Amicable agreements normally keep legal costs down. Around 3500 solicitors are members of the Solicitors' Family Law Association, which aims to help parting couples settle as cheaply and painlessly as possible.

The family home

There are various options you could take over the family home:

- Sell the home and divide the proceeds between you. This is unlikely to be a good option if you have children, because unless you have enough capital to buy a new home adequate for your family needs, you may be forced into one that is too small. Indeed, you may not be left with enough to buy a new home at all.
- Postpone the sale of the home until your children are no longer dependent. Under this arrangement, you stay in the family home, which is sold when your kids grow up. At that stage, the proceeds are divided between you and your former husband. This arrangement is often suggested by solicitors. But it may cause you problems in the future if you don't have enough money then to buy out your ex-spouse's share or to buy a new home.
- Buy out your ex-husband's share now. If you can afford to do this, it may well be the best option, because it provides

stability for you and your children. Talk to your lender about having your ex-husband's name taken off the deeds, and taking over the full mortgage yourself. Lenders may not allow you to take on the full mortgage if they do not believe you are capable of meeting the repayments.
- Handing over the home to one partner. This will only happen in very rare cases, for instance if your husband has far greater resources than you and you clearly have a much greater need for the home.

Staying put

If you want to stay in the family home, speak to your lender as soon as possible about what arrangements will be made for paying the mortgage. Bear in mind if you have a joint mortgage, you are liable for the full payments yourself if your ex-husband will not pay up. If your mortgage is in arrears, try to reach an agreement with your lender as soon as possible to avoid repossession.

Your income

It is obviously very important to get as much income as you can for yourself and your children, especially if you have not been working outside the home.

- You may be able to reach an agreement with your partner over how much maintenance he should pay you, or you can apply to the court for a maintenance order.
- If you are separated from your husband but not yet divorced and you are on Income Support, he must pay you maintenance at risk of being prosecuted. But this liability ends when you divorce.
- As soon as you separate, find out whether you are entitled to any social security benefits. Whether or not you are working, single mothers can claim One Parent Benefit at £6.30 a week (1995/6 figures) in addition to Child Benefit.

Tax matters

Your tax situation will change as a result of divorce, so it is important to notify your tax office.

- It is most likely that your ex-husband was getting the £1720 Married Couples' Allowance. If so, he will continue to receive it until the end of the tax year in which you split up. If you were receiving all or part of the allowance, you will also continue to receive it until the end of the tax year in which you split up.
- You can claim an Additional Personal Allowance of £1720 if you are bringing up a child or children on your own. Tax relief is granted at 15 per cent in 1995/6, so its value is £258. You can continue to claim so long as you have a child under 16, even if you live with a new partner, but you lose the allowance if you remarry.
- If both of you buy a new home, you are both entitled to Mortgage Interest Relief at Source or MIRAS on the interest on the first £30,000 of the loan. MIRAS is granted at 15 per cent in 1995/6.
- You do not have to pay tax on any maintenance payments your ex-husband makes to you, unless they fall under 'old rules' abolished in the Finance Act of 1988.

Child Support

The controversial new Child Support Agency was set up to deal with the problem of 'absent fathers' who do not pay proper maintenance for their children. Any single mother, whether she was married or not, can apply to the CSA for a maintenance assessment against the 'absent parent'.

Single mothers who are receiving means-tested benefits such as Income Support or Family Credit must apply to the CSA for a maintenance assessment, unless doing so would cause 'harm or undue distress', for example if your ex-husband is violent.

If you refuse to co-operate for any other reason, your benefits will be reduced.

Single mothers should make sure they have sufficient life insurance to look after their children in case anything happens. If you can afford it, you might also consider taking out permanent health insurance to cover you if you are ill and unable to work.

Money management

Thankfully, the old social stereotype of the man taking sole control of the family finances is dying out. But some women still find themselves being forced to handle money for the first time when they divorce. And even though married women typically take care of day-to-day household finances, research by Pearl Assurance has shown that men still dominate major money decisions, and that many women continue to find finance intimidating.

Don't be afraid to ask for help and advice from your bank or mortgage lender.

If you have received a lump sum settlement from your ex-husband, it is important to make the best use of it. Seek independent financial advice. On divorce, you will have to unravel your joint finances. Tell your bank or building society to freeze any joint accounts and set up new ones in your own name.

Normally the proceeds are split half and half, unless you and your ex-husband specify otherwise. If you have run up any joint debts, you may be liable for the full amount if your husband defaults. See Chapters 6 and 7 for more details.

On divorce, you will want to make a new will to reflect your changed circumstances. Divorce does not completely cancel a will but can cause serious complications, so it is vital to make a new one.

More information

The Solicitors' Family Law Association has a database of members:

>PO Box 302
>Orpington
>BR6 8QX
>Tel: 01689 850227

The Financial Forum for Women publishes free factsheets on *Separation and Divorce* and *Being a Single Parent*, tel: 0800 590682.

The Consumers' Association publishes an excellent book, The *Which? Guide to Divorce*, available from the Which? Bookshop, 359–361 Euston Road, London NW1, or tel: 0800 252100.

Relate (National Marriage Guidance)
Herbert Gray College
Little Church Street
Rugby
CV21 3AP
Tel: 01788 573241

National Council for One Parent Families
255 Kentish Town Road
London NW5 2LX
Tel: 0171-267 1361

Child Support Agency Helpline, tel: 0345 133133. Calls are charged at local rates.

DSS Helpline: 0800 666555, Northern Ireland: 0800 616757, Welsh speakers: 0800 289011.

The Inland Revenue publishes some helpful leaflets, available from tax offices: IR92, *Tax — A Guide for One Parent Families*, and IR 93, *Separation, Divorce and Maintenance Payments.* See also leaflet NI 95, *National Insurance for Divorced Women*, available from Benefits Agencies.

Appendix
More help and advice

Sources of further information and help are listed at the ends of the relevant chapters. There are, however, useful places to turn for general guidance.

General financial planning guidance

National & Provincial Building Society runs a free, unbiased information facility, Financial Services for Women. It has a free telephone enquiry service and a range of free booklets on tax, savings, pensions, wills and inheritance, along with a starter guide, the Essential Money Guide for Women. Contact:

Consumer Services Dept. FSW
National & Provincial Building Society
Provincial House
Bradford BD1 1NL
Tel: 0800 600200

The Financial Forum for Women was set up by the N&P and the National Council of Women to raise women's awareness about finance and help them cope with financial responsibilities. It publishes a range of free factsheets, including ones on starting work, being at home, divorce and separation, being a single parent, part-time work and retirement. Tel: 0800 590682.

Financial advice

Most women will want to seek advice from a financial expert before making a major investment decision. Advisers fall into two categories: independent financial advisers who should recommend you the best product on the whole market, and tied agents or company representatives who can only offer you a product from their own company's range.

Always ask the adviser which sort he or she is. Most financial journalists and commentators believe it is better to go to an independent adviser.

You will not normally be asked to write a cheque to pay for the advice. But that doesn't mean it's free — advisers earn their living through commissions on anything they sell you.

Both sorts of adviser are paid by commission which is taken out of the money you invest. It means an adviser might be tempted to recommend you an unsuitable product just because it pays him a high commission, or to sell you something you don't need at all.

To avoid this and increase your chances of genuinely unbiased advice, you can go to an adviser who charges a fee.

Financial advisers and investment companies ought to be authorised by the appropriate regulator. For most of the firms you deal with, the regulator will be the Personal Investment Authority. You can check whether a firm is authorised to do business by ringing the Securities and Investments Board Register on 0171-929 3652.

For a list of independent financial advisers in your area, contact: IFA Promotions, tel: 0117 971 1177.

You can get a list of fee-charging independent financial advisers from: The Money Management National Register of Independent Fee-based Advisers, c/o Matrix Data Ltd, Freepost 22 (SW1565), London W1E 7EZ, tel: 01272 769444.

Complaints

There are several independent ombudsmen you can turn to if you have a complaint and reach deadlock with the firm concerned. You must have exhausted the firm's own complaints procedures before the ombudsman can help.

All can order the firms to make you an award, up to a given ceiling, often £50,000 or £100,000.

The Banking Ombudsman
70 Gray's Inn Road
London WC1X 8NB
Tel: 0171-404 9944

The Building Societies Ombudsman
Grosvenor Gardens House
35–37 Grosvenor Gardens
London SW1X 7AW
Tel: 0171-931 0044

The Insurance Ombudsman Bureau
135 Park Street
London SE1 9EA
Tel: 0171 928 7600

The Occupational Pensions Advisory Service (OPAS) will deal with disputes about both company and personal pensions. If OPAS cannot sort it out, the problem may be referred to the Pensions Ombudsman.

OPAS
11 Belgrave Road
London SW1V 1RB
Tel: 0171-233 8080

The Pensions Ombudsman is at the same address.

Solicitors' Complaints Bureau
Victoria Court
8 Dormer Place
Leamington Spa
Warwickshire CU32 5AE
Tel: 01926 820082

Investments

The lead regulator for investment firms is the Securities and Investments Board (SIB). SIB delegates powers to a number of other watchdog. The Personal Investment Authority is the watchdog for firms carrying out retail business with the public, and is the one you are most likely to come across. The Securities and Futures Authority regulates stockbrokers. All have independent arrangements for dealing with investor complaints that cannot be resolved with the firm concerned.

Securities and Investments Board
Gavrelle House
2–14 Bunhill Row
London EC1Y 8RA
Tel: 0171-638 1240

Personal Investment Authority
3 Royal Exchange Buildings
London EC3V 3NL
Tel: 0171-929 0072

Securities & Futures Authority
The Cotton Centre
Cottons Lane
London SE1 2QB
Tel: 0171-378 9000

Compensation

The SIB runs an Investors' Compensation Scheme which will pay out if you lose money through an authorised investment firm which goes bust or is fraudulent. It will not pay out just because you buy an investment which performs badly leading to a loss.

The maximum payout is £48,000 — full protection for the first £30,000 you invest, and 90 per cent of the next £20,000.

In the extremely unlikely event of a building society going bust, there is a compensation scheme which will pay 90 per cent of the first £20,000 of savings.

If a bank goes under, you are covered for 75 per cent of the first £20,000 invested with it.

Investment-linked insurance products are covered by the Policyholders Protection Act. You will receive at least 90 per cent of the amount guaranteed when the company went bust.

The Investors' Compensation Scheme
Gavrelle House
2–14 Bunhill Row
London EC1Y 8RA
Tel: 0171-628 8820

Benefits

Freeline Social Security on 0800 666555; Northern Ireland: 0800 521360. Welsh speakers: 0800 289011.

Index

benefits for mothers 92
borrowing money 45–52
   bad references 49–50
   cost of credit 46
   credit insurance 47–8
   dealing with debt 50
   joint borrowings 48–9
   longer-term loans 47
   options 45
   short-term 46–7
   more information 51
business plans, self-employment and 105–6

capital gains tax 29–30
career breaks, pensions and 67–8
children, financial planning for 91–4
   benefits for mothers 92
   first steps 91–2
   protecting your family 92
   saving for children 93–4
   school fees 92–3
   more information 94
   see also maternity rights
combining work and home 99–104
   flexible working 100–1
   part-time work 100
   working from home 101
   more information 102–3

common law marriage *see* living together
company pensions 59–62
   and career breaks 67–8
   final salary schemes 60
   hybrid schemes 61
   money purchase schemes 60–1
compensation, investors' 120
complaints procedures 118–19
credit *see* borrowing money

debt, dealing with 50
deposit-based PPPs 65
divorce, dealing with 109–15
   child support 112–13
   the family home 110–11
   financial settlement 109–10
   money management 113
   pensions and 75–8
   staying put 111
   tax matters 112
   your income 111–12
   more information 114–15

employment, women and 33–6
   combining work and home 99–104
   flexible working 100–1
   part-time work 100
   working from home 101
   more information 102–3

equal opportunities 35
equal pay 33–5
job pensions 59–62
  and career breaks 67–8
  final salary schemes 60
  hybrid schemes 61
  money purchase schemes 60–1
job-changers' pensions 71–3
  leaving where it is 71
  moving to new employer 71–2
  transfer to insurance company 72–3
  more information 73
maternity rights 95–8
  maternity benefits 96–7
  telling your employer 97–8
  more information 98
and tax 29
more information 36
endowment policies 24
equal opportunities 35
  equal pay 33–5
  equal pension ages 56–7

family planning, financial 91–4
  benefits for mothers 92
  first steps 91–2
  protecting your family 92
  saving for children 93–4
  school fees 92–3
  more information 94
  see also maternity rights
final salary schemes 60
financial advice/guidance, general 117–18
flexible working 100–1
friendly society plans 24–5
full-time wives/mothers 68

gilts 25

home, buying your own 37–44
  buying costs 40–1
  divorce and 110–11
  finding a home 37–8
  home responsibilities protection 55
  living together and 80–1
  mortgages 38–43
    choosing a 38–9
    joint 42
    problems with 42–3
    variable/fixed rate interest 40
  moving in 41
  more information 43
hybrid schemes, pension 61

inheritance tax 30
insurance, living together and 82
investment income 14, 119–20
  see also savings accounts/ strategies

job-changers, pensions and 71–3
  leaving where it is 71
  moving to new employer 71–2
  transfer to insurance company 72–3
  more information 73
joint savings/investments 87–8

life insurance cover 89
living together 79–84
  insurance 82
  making a will 81–2
  and pensions 83
  savings 83

Index

tax and benefits 82–3
your home 80–1
more information 84
loans *see* borrowing money; mortgages

marriage, money and 85–90
  joint savings/investments 87–8
  life insurance cover 89
  making a will 88
  preparing for 86
  tax and 86–7
  more information 89
  see also divorce, dealing with; family planning, financial; living together
maternity rights 95–8
  maternity benefits 96–7
  telling your employer 97–8
  for working women 95–6
    maternity leave 96
    while pregnant 95
  more information 98
money purchase schemes 60–1
mortgages 38–43
  choosing a 38–9
  divorce and 110–11
  joint 42
  problems with 42–3
  variable/fixed rate interest 40

National Savings 18–20

ombudsmen 118–19

part-time work 100
pensions 53–8
  boosting 68–9
  and career breaks 67–8

divorce and 75–8
early retirement 69–70
equal pension ages 56–7
full-time wives/mothers 68
home responsibilities protection 55
living together and 83
personal pension plans 63–6, 68, 69
SERPS 56, 65–6
state pensions 54–5, 67
tips for job-changers 71–3
with your job 59–62, 67–8
more information 57
pensions and partners 75–8
personal equity plans (PEPs) *see* stocks and shares
personal pensions *see* pensions
personal tax allowances *see* taxation
pre-nuptial agreements 86

retirement *see* pensions
risk and reward 12–13

savings strategies 11–15
  accounts and investments 13, 17–20
    investment income 14
    National Savings 18–20
    tax exempt accounts 18
    tax on 17, 29
    more information 20
  aims 11–12
  living together and 83
  marriage and 87–8
  maximising savings 14–15
  risk and reward 12–13
  saving for children 93–4

school fees 92–3
Securities and Investments Board (SIB) 119–20
self-employment, women and 105–8
  business plans 105–6
  tax, VAT and financial planning 106–7
  more information 107–8
  see also combining work and home
short-term loans 46–7
State Earnings Related Pension Scheme (SERPS) 56
  contracting out 65–6
state pensions 54–5
  and career breaks 67
stocks and shares 21–6
  endowment policies 24
  friendly society plans 24–5
  gilts 25
  personal equity plans (PEPs) 23–4
  unit and investment trusts 22–3
  more information 26

taxation 27–32
  capital gains 29–30
  declaring 30–1
  divorce and 112
  employment and 29
  income tax
    rates/bands 28–9
    on savings/investments 29
  inheritance tax 30
  living together and 82–3
  marriage and 86–7
  older women's/couples' allowances 28
  on savings 17
  self-employment and 106–7
  tax exempt accounts 18
  tax saving tips 31–2
  tax-free allowances 27–8
  more information 32

unit and investment trusts 22–3
unit-linked PPPs 64–5

will, making a 81–2, 88
with profits PPPs 64
work and home, combining *see* combining work and home